HUNGER AND DISCIPLESHIP

A Study and Action Resource
by Vicki Ross

The World Hunger Committee
Reorganized Church of Jesus Christ of
Latter Day Saints

ACKNOWLEDGMENTS

The World Hunger Committee wishes to thank the following for their assistance in the production of this resource:

- Robert E. Kent, Editor, Zionic Relations Office
- Art Department, Herald House, layout and design
- Office of Graphic Arts, cover design

TABLE OF CONTENTS

FOREWORD

Most of us who read this book are fortunate enough to live in a culture which provides us with more than enough resources to lead comfortable and fulfilling lives. We may often take for granted the fact that we have plenty of food, shelter, energy and security, as well as many good relationships which nurture and sustain us throughout our lives. We can truthfully say that God has blessed us abundantly.

It may come as a shock to many of us, therefore, to learn that in contrast to our comfort and affluence many peoples of the world live in abject poverty and deprivation, without having even the most basic means for human survival. In the midst of the complex problem of world hunger is the fact that rich nations and affluent citizens consume far more resources than are necessary for their survival, while others do not have enough to keep either themselves or their children alive.

But we should not be so much preoccupied with the seriousness of the problem or feel guilty about our place in it, as we should be busy working for solutions which address the basic causes of the problem. An approach to the solution may begin by first recognizing what those resources are which we have and others do not, and *why* they do not have them. As Christians, may we then ask ourselves what it is we value in life. Do we value our own comfort so much that we would prevent our less fortunate brothers and sisters from sharing in it? Or do we feel, as Jesus once suggested, that when we help those who hunger or thirst, i.e., when "we do it to one of the least of these," we do it to him? Can we begin to change our point of view from one of "mine" to one of "ours"? And can we begin to see ourselves as a world community, instead of isolated pockets of rich and poor? If so, how may we do this?

Dr. Vicki Ross, in her book *Hunger and Discipleship*, has provided a study and action resource which can be a valuable tool for making our initial response—as congregations and individuals—to this challenging problem. She begins by identifying and analyzing the seriousness and complexity of the problem. Then by looking to the scriptures to discover some of the insights which come to us through them, she provides us with a base for a Christian response to the problem. We believe that the Restoration concept of stewardship also has much to offer as we consider potential solutions. It is from this point of view that Dr. Ross provides us with a variety of strategies and activities we can employ as we commit ourselves and become equipped for action.

It is hoped that by studying the complexity of the problem of world hunger, Christian disciples everywhere will feel the need to respond affirmatively. Thus, all study will ideally be translated into action.

But there is more to this simple framework than meets the eye. Reorganized Latter Day Saints and other Christian disciples have experienced something in their lives which has caused them to seek an active relationship with God and Christ. Because of these "faith encounters" we know that God lives and that God's son, Jesus, is the revelation out of which we understand and experience God's redeeming love. We know this because our faith experiences have led us to conclude it. The impact of the Christ on our lives has been redemptive. Our lives have been changed as we have allowed the workings of the gospel to penetrate all aspects of our existence. By living the gospel, then, we effectively become new creations, with confidence in the present and hope for the future.

This knowledge is crucial as we confront the problem of world hunger. We might understand all there is to know about world hunger, its causes, its complexity, and potential avenues for eradicating it from the face of the earth, but we need more. As Christian disciples who would work to alleviate the conditions of world hunger, we should strive to make real a vision of the gospel and God's love which is redemptive and empowering. Our message to those suffering from the effects of chronic hunger should be one of new possibilities, of new beginnings, of hope. We should see our mission to such persons in light of the cross of Jesus, and be willing to help carry the burden of their suffering. We may then be willing to examine ways our life-styles may be adjusted toward eliminating unnecessary consumption and committing our resources in pursuit of justice, reconciliation, and human development. As we do so, we will no longer enjoy our own health and prosperity at the expense of other human beings. Our corporate and personal positions must be that all persons are of infinite worth. Whatever happens to other persons affects us, since we are all parts of God's creation. We are bound together by the priceless gift of life, a gift made more valuable by the sacrificial life of Jesus Christ.

We trust that readers will approach the material in *Hunger and Discipleship* with these thoughts in mind, and would challenge all who read and study this resource to take seriously its call for Christian discipleship. Perhaps such a foundation will cause us to be even more committed to alleviating world hunger during our lifetime.

World hunger is a problem which threatens the very foundations upon which the civilized world rests. But in a more personal way, it is a problem which ravages the lives of millions of children the world over, even in the most affluent of nations. Thus, when we look into the faces of our children, we are reminded of the other face of hunger—those children who will never experience the joys we experience.

There is a need for all to engage in the effort to overcome the problems of world hunger and human development. It is the hope of the First Presidency and the World Hunger Committee that those who study this resource will be stimulated to join in the struggle so that the legacy left to succeeding generations will be one of abundance, joy, and fulfillment.

THE FIRST PRESIDENCY

Wallace B. Smith

THE WORLD HUNGER COMMITTEE

W. Wallace Smith

INTRODUCTION

"How can God allow so much suffering to go on in the world?" asked a friend of mine after a recent presentation on world hunger. Her question is one which many people have struggled to answer. The fact that there is extreme deprivation and suffering of millions of people in the world is outrageous! How can we believe in a God of love when so many of God's children exist in conditions of unspeakable poverty and wretchedness?

A dramatic answer to this question is offered by Jack Nelson in his book, *Hunger for Justice.*

As I walked through the streets of Calcutta, the poverty so enraged me that I wanted to scream at God. How could God tolerate such suffering? Then I came to a painful realization: in the suffering of the poor God was screaming at me, in fact at all of us and at our institutions and social systems that cause and perpetuate hunger, poverty, and inequality. *

We often tend to blame God for misfortune which we bring upon ourselves. The poverty and hunger which afflict the lives of millions today are not God's doing. They are the result of human-created systems and orders, of human action and inaction. If hunger is to be eliminated, we must acknowledge our responsibility for its existence and set about making the changes which can overcome it. Most of all, we need to recognize that hunger *can* be eliminated if we are serious enough about doing so.

One of the most difficult, yet promising, tasks of our day involves bringing ourselves to that degree of

---

* Jack A. Nelson, *Hunger for Justice: The Politics of Food and Faith* (Maryknoll, New York: Orbis Books, 1980) p. vii.

compassion and outrage which will result in real commitment to the elimination of injustice, poverty, and hunger. The way in which we perceive the problem, and the value which we place upon those who are its victims, will largely determine our response. We need a conversion of conscience which will help us see the world through God's eyes. In that condition of enlightenment we may begin to recognize that it is Christ who appears to us in the poor and hungry—just as he said—and him we supply when we help "the least of these" (Matthew 25:41). He is indeed crying to us in the suffering of the poor, and asking how much longer we will allow their cries to go unheard.

Sometimes we are encouraged to act ourselves as we see the exemplary action of others. One of the most moving examples I have seen of response to the needs of the poor occurred in a small rural village in the Philippines. My son and I were attending a Sunday morning worship service with the Saints in Simimbaan. At that time the average annual income of these families was around $200. They lived in bamboo huts without electricity, water, or even the simplest comforts.

At the close of the service the pastor announced that an offering would be received "for the poor who are suffering in Haiti." The basket was passed and these people, of such meager means themselves, shared their pesos with "the poor."

That kind of response to hunger—unreserved and unconditional—can change our world. It needs to take many forms that will achieve social, economic, and political change. It deserves our wisest and best efforts. The life of Jesus calls us to live our lives on behalf of others, to measure our faith by our response, to match our concern with commitment, our awareness with action.

This resource is designed as a preparation for action. It is hoped that increased understanding of the existence and causes of world hunger will lead persons into a program of personal and corporate responses.

This resource is offered with the hope that concern for the poor and hungry will lead us to acts of justice, love and peace, in keeping with the example of our Lord who "though he was rich, yet for [our] sakes he became poor, that [we] through his poverty might be rich" (II Corinthians 8:9).

Vicki Ross, Ph.D.
February, 1982

USER'S GUIDE

This resource may be used for both individual and group study. It includes a Teacher's Guide for those who lead group study.

An organizational session is suggested as a means of introducing the resource for the group setting. It includes a pretest which encourages participants to think about the world as a whole. The first three chapters of the resource describe the dimensions and basic causes of hunger. *It is important that the reader study this material carefully in order that the responses stimulated by these and the ensuing chapters shall address the causes, rather than only the symptoms, of hunger.*

The study is composed of six chapters, each of which is based on the following general format:

1) Theme article
2) Reflection and Discussion Questions
3) For Further Exploration
4) Action Suggestions
5) Worship Suggestions
6) Teacher's Guide
    a) Learning Objectives
    b) Overview of Chapter
    c) Recommended Procedure
    d) Resources Needed
7) Additional Resources*
8) Notes

---

* Most of these will have to be ordered by mail. Try to allow several weeks lead time to ensure their availability at the time when you will need them.

TEACHER'S GUIDE FOR INITIAL PLANNING SESSION

Objectives

At this session participants will

1. plan class meeting dates, time, and location.
2. receive individual copies of the study resource.
3. complete and discuss the "Hunger Pretest."
4. start thinking about the world as a whole and how people are affected by hunger.
5. share their personal expectations for the course.
6. be given study/worship assignments for Chapter 1.

Overview of Session One

Session One may be used as an organizational meeting. The group should decide upon dates, time, and place for class sessions. Distribute copies of the study resource and review the Introduction and chapter titles. Each chapter includes discussion questions, action suggestions, and an outline for worship. Decide whether your group would prefer to use the suggested worship to close or to open each session.

Ask students to complete the "Hunger Pretest." This is an exercise to start them thinking about the world as a whole and the ways in which people are affected by hunger. Students are not expected to get all of the answers right.

Answer Key to the Hunger Pretest: (1) a; (2) a; (3) b; (4) b; (5) a; (6) a; (7) d; (8) c; (9) c; (10) a.

Follow the pretest with a brief discussion of the questions which follow. Question three may be used as an assignment for the next session. In addition, ask students to read Chapter 1 and be prepared to discuss the "Reflection and Discussion Questions."

Conclude the session by asking participants to share what they hope to gain from the course. Close with prayer. Ask three students to participate in the worship for the next session by completing the statement "If we are truly to practice our faith we will. . . ." These thoughts should be related to the suggested scriptures.

HUNGER PRETEST
"Our World: Find Out What You Know"

1. How many people are there in the world?

   a. 4 billion   c. 8 billion

   b. 1 billion   d. 10 billion   1. _____

2. One out of ____people in the world never has enough food for good health.

   a. eight   c. two

   b. ten   d. fifteen   2. _____

3. ____percent of developing country residents (except China) live without adequate water supplies.

   a. 45   c. 88

   b. 62   d. 74   3. _____

4. The average protein intake per person in the United States is 106 grams each day. In Bangladesh it is

   a. 60 grams   c. 70 grams

   b. 40 grams   d. 90 grams   4. _____

5. Some 900 million people in the developing nations subsist on ____ a year.

   a. $40 to $80   c. $500 to $600

   b. $100 to $150 d. $5 to $10   5. _____

6. The average life expectancy for men and women in the United States is 73 years. In Bolivia it is

   a. 52   c. 62

   b. 55   d. 70   6. _____

7. The infant mortality rate (deaths under 1 year of age per 1,000 live births) is 18 in the United States. In Tanzania it is

   a. 25   c. 52

   b. 100   d. 162   7. _____

8. Poor people in the developing countries are paying up to ____ percent of their earnings for food (subsistence diets).

   a. 50   c. 85

   b. 25   d. 95   8. _____

9. According to the World Bank, in some 80 countries, just over 3 percent of the people own or control _____ percent of the farmland.

    a. 20   c. 50

    b. 35   d. 80   9. _____

10. What percent of the U.S. Gross National Product goes to foreign development assistance?

    a. less than 1% c. about 5%

    b. about 25% d. about 10%   10. _____

(The answers to the pretest are found on p. 13.)

For Discussion
1. What answer from the quiz was the most surprising to you? Why?
2. Draw a conclusion about the world in which we live from any five of the questions and answers above.
3. Get three people *not* in your class to take this quiz. Then compare their answers with yours. What similarities and differences did you notice?
4. Has this experience provided you with helpful insights into the serious problem of world hunger? Share one or two of these with a friend.

CHAPTER 1

OUR HUNGRY WORLD

"There's a great big beautiful tomorrow, waiting at the end of every day; there's a great big beautiful tomorrow, and tomorrow is just a dream away!" So run the lines of a catchy tune that introduces one of the exhibits at Disney World in Orlando, Florida. For most people in the world, such a rosy tomorrow seems very unlikely. Rather, tomorrow will bring increased tragedy and suffering for millions unless some very creative dreams are born and courageous people translate them into reality. How can we become such dreamers and doers?

The first step to successful problem solving involves defining the problem. Unless we define the problem realistically and precisely, there is little hope that we can solve it. This is true of world hunger. If we are to bring about changes which will eliminate hunger, we must spend some time learning about the nature of hunger. Where does it exist? How many people are hungry? What are the effects of hunger? Are there any linkages between hunger in some parts of the world and excessive food consumption in other parts? *Why* are people hungry? Let us begin by examining some of the answers to these questions.

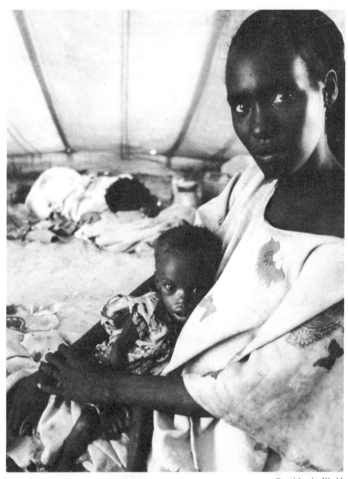

Bread for the World

Undernutrition

More than one billion people—one fourth of the human race—suffer from constant hunger or "undernutrition." Approximately 10,000 people die each day either from the lack of enough food to sustain life or the right food to ward off disease. One out of four children in developing countries dies before the age of five—mostly from nutrition-related causes. Many who survive are the victims of recurrent infections, stunted growth, and brain damage.

Constant undernutrition results when people consume fewer calories and less protein than their bodies require to lead active, healthy lives. Undernutrition is "an invisible crisis, a daily tragedy that deprives hundreds of millions of the right to realize their genetic potential—their birthright."[1] The weakness, inactivity, and suffering of millions who are deprived of an adequate diet effectively prevent the development of many countries, particularly in Asia, Africa, and Latin America.

In *Living Poor*, Mortiz Thomsen, a forty-eight-year-old farmer from the state of Washington, tells of his initial experience as a Peace Corps volunteer in a remote village of Ecuador. He was outraged by the apparent laziness of the villagers—until circumstances forced him to eat what they ate. Then he discovered why many of the world's farmers are able to work only three or four hours a day.[2] They are weak from hunger, often infested with parasites, and suffer frequent debilitating illnesses.

Thomsen also describes the desperation and heartbreak of parents whose children die of hunger:

During a drought people in a nearby village "were selling their children before they died of hunger; autopsies on the

**ones who had died revealed stomachs full of roots and dirt."
In his own village the birth of a stillborn child was occasion
for jubilant celebration, since it meant that someone had
become an *angelito* without all the suffering.[3]**

Such people as these, who were living a marginal
existence before the drought, cannot survive even a
minimal additional crisis. Unfortunately, this is not an
isolated case—millions around the globe share a similar
plight.

Despite the magnitude of the continuing tragedy, today
the world hunger problem seldom receives publicity.
Famine in some areas may be reported, but chronic
hunger is a back-page story, or a nonstory, even though
millions of lives are at stake. It kills silently and indirectly
by decreasing a population's resistance to infection and
disease. Many deaths attributed to disease are actually a
result of malnutrition. Its victims are without the physical,
economic, and political power to make their need known
and their powerlessness perpetuates their hunger. Children under five make up over half of the world's malnourished population, and significantly more women are
affected than men.

Affluent Malnutrition

While millions in the developing world suffer the
ravages of undernutrition, those in industrialized
countries are victims of another form of malnutrition. The
excessive consumption of rich, highly refined foods has
led to *over*nutrition—a result of the "affluent diet." Those
suffering from overnutrition consume large amounts of
animal proteins and fats, highly refined flour and sugar,
and commercially prepared foods. These are substituted

for the traditional whole grains, tubers (roots), fresh fruits, and vegetables.

The affluent diet has come under increasing scrutiny as research has linked it with a high incidence of degenerative diseases. Leading killers among affluent populations are such diseases as coronary heart disease, diabetes, diverticulosis (an intestinal disorder), and bowel cancer. Coronary heart disease, once a rare affliction even among the aged, now accounts for one in every three deaths in the United States. One in four persons in industrialized countries develops cancer. Current evidence relates as much as 50 percent of all cancer in women and one-third of all cancer in men to diet. Growing evidence suggests a causal link to high-fat, low-fiber diets.[4]

Diabetes has risen from the twenty-seventh most common cause of death in the United States in 1900 to fifth; when deaths from complications are added, it is third. Dr. Cahill, Chief of Joslin Diabetes Research Center in Boston, Massachusetts, states: "The greatest portion of diabetes . . . here in the United States is frankly due . . . to overnutrition. A person 20 percent overweight is more than twice as likely to develop diabetes as a person of normal weight."[5]

A Complex Relationship

Is there a relationship between the malnutrition of the poor and the malnutrition of the rich? It has been suggested that one is the outgrowth, or the natural complement, of the other. If we could divide present food supplies evenly, there would be enough food for

everyone. But the uneven distribution of the world's wealth has contributed to the accumulation of food supplies and other resources among the wealthy, thus diverting them from the poor. The maldistribution of the world's food supplies is in proportion to the inequitable distribution of the world's wealth and power.

A comparison of the Gross National Product (GNP—the sum of all of a country's goods and services produced in a year) per capita among the following nations presents the extent of the contrast that exists between rich and poor countries. If we divide the total GNP by the number of people in the country, we can arrive at a per capita (per person) GNP. (See Chart A)

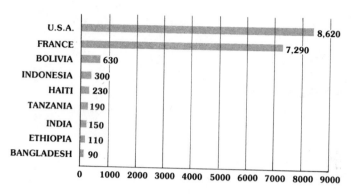

CHART A:
Gross National Product Per Capita
(U.S. Dollars, 1977)[6]

One way we can compare the available food supplies within different nations is to calculate the daily per capita *calorie* supply. This is done by dividing the calorie equivalent of available food supplies in a country by its total population. This is a measure of total calorie *supply,* not actual consumption. Therefore, large numbers of a population may fall *far below* and others *far above* the calorie supply available, according to purchasing power. The minimum number of calories required for normal adults is 2,700. This varies somewhat according to how active they are. Chart B compares the food supplies available in several different nations.

The adequacy of a population's diet is reflected in the life expectancy of a country. Life expectancy indicates the number of years persons born into that country may be expected to live given the mortality risks prevailing for a cross section of the population. (See Chart C)

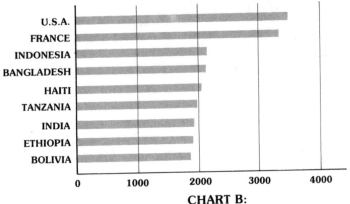

CHART B:
Daily Per Capita Calorie Supply[7]

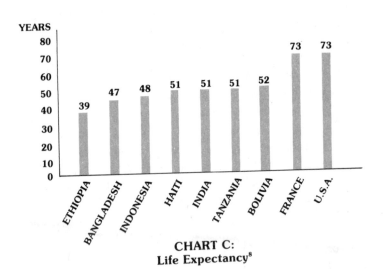

CHART C:
Life Expectancy[8]

The wealth of a country has much to do with the educational opportunities that are available to its citizens. Chart D indicates the percentage of young people of secondary school (high school) age who are actually enrolled in secondary school in each country.

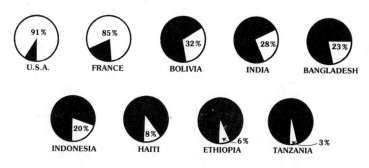

CHART D: PERCENTAGE OF AGE GROUP ENROLLED IN SECONDARY SCHOOL[9]

Social researchers have developed an index that gives a broader and more accurate picture of conditions within a country than that given by GNP. This index is called the "Physical Quality of Life Index" (PQLI). Each country's PQLI is based on an average of its index rates for life expectancy, infant mortality, and literacy. (See Chart E)

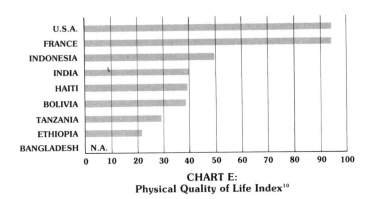

CHART E:
Physical Quality of Life Index[10]

These charts may help us to see how *wealth, food supply,* and *life expectancy* are tied together, and how they impact other factors like *education*.

Some hunger pockets also exist within industrialized nations. For example, there are some 25 million persons in the United States who are not able to purchase adequate diets. One example is found among some ethnic groups who suffer from hunger far above their percentage of the population. Although they represent less than 12 percent of the population, Blacks make up 30 percent of the poor in this country. The Native American and Native Alaskan populations are among the most impoverished and malnourished ethnic groups in the United States. Their annual family income averages $1,900, the lowest of all ethnic groups. The U.S. Bureau of Indian Affairs reports unemployment among native

Americans living on reservations at 40 to 50 percent. Food costs for reservation Indians average 28 percent higher than for urban consumers.[11]

The elderly are among the hungry in the United States, as well as those who live in depressed areas like Appalachia and the rural South. Thirteen percent of the 25 million U.S. poor are over sixty-five. Stories of the elderly eating dog food, of children no longer able to buy school lunches, and of a rash of petty thievery in supermarkets by people who have never before stolen anything show the human face of the domestic food problem.

Most of the approximately three million migrant farm workers in the United States are also among the hungry. Because they are constantly on the move, they often fail to qualify for government food programs. Several studies have shown high rates of malnutrition, growth retardation, anemia, and rickets among farm workers' children. The life expectancy of migrants has been estimated at forty-nine years compared with the national average of seventy-three.[12]

Conclusion

Although some poverty and hunger does exist in the United States and in other industrialized nations, it is clear that it is not the same in scope and intensity as that in Third World countries. For example, the poor in the United States spend an estimated 40 percent of their income on food while millions in the developing world must spend 85 percent of their income for food and still find that inadequate to meet minimum nutritional requirements. Also, food aid programs and other benefits—such as housing subsidies, Medicaid and Medicare—have alleviated some of the worst aspects of poverty for perhaps half of the poor in the United States.

U.S. citizens, however, face the temptation to ignore hunger on a global scale in favor of focusing upon domestic needs. The two need to be dealt with simultaneously as two complexly interrelated factors. As one author states, "We cannot deal with our international responsibility unless we face our domestic needs. However, to use the U.S. domestic situation as an excuse *not* to face our international responsibility is to open ourselves to a horrendous future."[13]

Reflection and Discussion Questions

1. Do you know anyone who is really hungry or suffering from *under*nutrition? Do you know anyone who suffers from *over*nutrition? Compare and discuss your feelings about each of these conditions.

2. List three factors that would, in your opinion, explain the differences in per capita GNP between the countries listed in Chart A.

_____

_____

_____

3. Compare the chart on calorie supply (Chart B) with that on life expectancy (Chart C) (p. 26). Compare the chart on PQLI (Chart E) with the chart on numbers enrolled in secondary school (Chart D) (pp. 27-28). What conclusions can you draw from these comparisons?

4. Why do you think hunger exists in your country? Record your thoughts and share them with someone.

_____

_____

_____

_____

5. The following note appeared on the front page of the February 24, 1977, *Wall Street Journal* (a daily U.S. business newspaper).

   Perfect Diet? A major food company is said to be working on several new ways of eliminating the intake of calories. One method involves an additive that prevents digestion. Another is based on foods impossible to digest, such as cellulose. Test marketing is expected before 1979, a trade source says.
   a. What is your reaction to this?
   b. Would you buy such a product? Why or why not?

For Further Exploration

In September of 1973, the governor of Illinois (U.S.A.) proclaimed Illinois to be a world state, and its citizens world citizens, whose responsibilities extend beyond the boundaries of Illinois. Governor Walker said:

This nuclear age has provided the foundation for world citizenship and for the establishment of permanent peace based on world law. Only through world cooperation can we recognize the common interest of humankind, free it from the curses of avarice and war, hunger and pollution, and convert the resources of the world to its service.

1. What is your reaction to the governor's action?
2. Do you consider yourself a citizen of the world? Why or why not? What responsibility do your feel for the rest of the world?
3. What factors are making people more conscious of being part of a global society? List several.

_____   _____

_____   _____

_____   _____

4. What factors hinder people from such a state of consciousness?
5. How does the Christian gospel encourage us to think in terms of a global society?
6. If we begin to think in terms of a global society, what kinds of responsibilities would various nations have to each other? Discuss.

Action Suggestions

1. The next time you watch TV take notes on the various food products that are advertised. List those that have high nutritional value. List those that may be considered only "empty calories" (food that is caloric but has little or no nutritional value). List those foods and/or nonfood commodities that may be considered actually harmful. After compiling your lists, note which one is the longest? Second longest? Shortest? On which list do most of the foods you eat belong?

High Nutrition Foods	Empty Calorie Foods	Harmful Foods

2. It has been observed that through the combined U.S. government PL-480 (Food for Peace) and CCC (Commodity Credit Corporation) programs, the United States has given $80 million in loans for tobacco purchases to the Philippines, a country where the people are suffering severe malnutrition. In 1980 Michael Barnes (Democrat, Maryland) introduced in the U.S. Congress anti-dumping legislation (House of Representatives Resolution 6587) which would "restrict the export of goods which have been found to be hazardous to the public health." Call or write your legislator and find out what has happened to this bill. Report to the group. What do you think of such proposed legislation?

3. Find out who the hungry people are in your community.* How can you help them?

_____

_____

_____

_____

_____

_____

_____

4. Discover whether there is a community food bank or food pantry in your town or city, and if so find out how your church can contribute. If not, find out whether your group might like to start one and ask other religious and civic groups to help. For further information contact: The Second Harvest Network, 1001 N. Central, Suite 303, Phoenix, Arizona, U.S.A., 85004.

---

* To get this information, contact local service organizations such as the local welfare office, the international or local Red Cross, Salvation Army, the local legal aid office, or agencies that work with migrants or ethnic groups.

Worship Suggestions

For a worship setting place upon a table a loaf of bread and a few spikes of grain. Consider together the symbolism of the plump, round kernels all joined together, all the same size, all a gift of the earth that we might eat. Consider the Source of life who has brought it forth. Consider the Source who has also brought us forth, and who feeds us with broken bread that we may feast upon eternal food which will satisfy our hunger forever. Eating that food makes us different, joins us with the Source of life and sends us forth to feed others. Reflect upon the call to go forth, acting on behalf of our hungry brothers and sisters while sharing the following scriptures:

Hereby perceive we the love of Christ, because he laid down his life for us; and we ought to lay down our lives for the brethren. But whoso hath this world's good, and seeth his brother have need, and shutteth up his bowels of compassion from him, how dwelleth the love of God in him? My little children, let us not love in word, neither in tongue only; but in deed and in truth. — I John 3:16-18

And the people asked him, saying, What shall we do then? He answered and said unto them, He that hath two coats, let him impart to him that hath none; and he that hath meat, let him do likewise. — Luke 3:15-16

If thou lovest me, thou shalt serve me and keep all my commandments. And behold, thou wilt remember the poor, and consecrate of thy properties for their support . . . and inasmuch as ye impart of your substance unto the poor, ye will do it unto me. — Doctrine and Covenants 42:8a-c

Ask three people to complete the following statement in a few sentences: "If we are truly to practice our faith we will. . . ." Close with prayer for those who hunger and for those who go forth to love "in deed and truth."

Teacher's Guide

Learning Objectives

At the close of this session participants will be able to

1. state approximately what proportion of the world's population is undernourished.
2. describe some of the effects of undernutrition/overnutrition.
3. describe what population groups are most affected by hunger.
4. identify geographic locations of the most extensive and severe incidences of hunger in the world.
5. identify several indicators of the uneven distribution of the world's resources.

Overview of Chapter 1

In Chapter 1 the author describes the dimensions of hunger and malnutrition in the world and the detrimental effects of overnutrition as a contrasting form of malnutrition. Data is presented that portray the realities of the uneven distribution of the world's wealth. Food supplies are concentrated in areas where purchasing power is greatest. Hunger pockets also exist within affluent nations, such as the United States, but it is suggested that this should not prevent developed nations from working to eradicate the extensive and severe poverty and hunger in the less-developed countries.

Recommended Procedure

1. Review briefly the content of Chapter 1.
2. Discuss the "Reflection and Discussion Questions" with the group (or in small groups). It would be helpful if the four charts mentioned in question three could be shown on an overhead projector or copied on newsprint and displayed so that the whole class could view them together.
3. Discuss the questions listed under "For Further Exploration." Help students to develop a world view. Help them to discover those factors which hinder them from developing such a perspective.
4. Ask for volunteers to carry out the "Action Suggestions," and to report at the next session.
5. Conclude the session with the "Worship Suggestions." The leader will need to be prepared to share the opening thoughts and read the suggested scriptures (or ask three members of the group to read them). Follow this with the brief sharing of those who have been asked to complete the statement "If we are truly to practice our faith we will. . . ." These thoughts should be related to the suggested scriptures. Close with prayer as suggested.

Resources Needed

Newsprint or overhead projector
Felt-tip markers
Small table for worship center
Loaf of bread (preferably home baked)
A few spikes of grain (wheat, oats, or barley)
Writing utensils

Additional Resources[*]

Films

"You May Have Heard," Filmstrip No. 1 from "A World Hungry" is an effective supplement to this session. "A World Hungry" is a five-part filmstrip series on hunger, its causes, solutions, and Christian responses. Available from Franciscan Communications Center, 1229 Santee Street, Los Angeles, California 90015. Also available from Audio-Visual Library, the Auditorium, Independence, MO 64051. Rental: $6.00 for all five filmstrips.

"The Faces of My Brother" and "The Face of Hunger," Maryknoll Film Libraries, Maryknoll Media Relations, Maryknoll, NY 10545. Depicts the reality of hunger. Free rental.

"Tilt," American Friends Service Committee, 1501 Cherry Street, Philadelphia, PA 19102. Rental: $5.00. Describes the way in which the world's wealth is shared, cartoon form. Also available from the Audio-Visual Library, the Auditorium. Rental: $7.00

Books

Arthur Simon, *Bread for the World*, Paulist Press, 1975, Chapter 1. Available from Bread for the World, 32 Union Square East, New York, NY 10003. Cost $3.50.

Barbara Howell, "Hungry in the USA," Bread for the World Background Paper No. 40, Bread for the World, 32 Union Square East, New York, NY 10003. Cost: free. Send stamped, self-addressed envelope.

---

[*] All addresses are in the United States of America unless otherwise indicated.

Erik Ekholm, "The Two Faces of Malnutrition," Worldwatch Paper 9, Worldwatch Institute, 1776 Massachusetts Avenue, NW, Washington, D.C. 20036. Cost $2.00.

Notes

1. Erik Ekholm, cited in U.S. Presidential Commission on World Hunger, *Overcoming World Hunger, The Challenge Ahead*, March 1980, p. 15.
2. Cited in Arthur Simon, *Bread for the World*, Paulist Press, 1975, pp. 3 and 4.
3. Ibid.
4. Erik Ekholm and Frank Record, "The Two Faces of Malnutrition," Worldwatch Paper 9, December 1976, pp. 40-42.
5. Ibid., p. 39.
6. World Development Report, World Bank, 1979.
7. Ibid.
8. Ibid.
9. Ibid. The 1976 percentage for the United States is actually the figure reported for 1975.
10. World Development Report, World Bank, 1979.
11. *Hunger Education/Action Manual*, National Council of Churches, August 1977, p. 15.
12. Barbara Howell, "Hungry in the U.S.A.," Bread for the World Background Paper No. 40, October 1979.
13. "Domestic and International Responsibility," *Dimensions of Hunger*, United Methodist Discipleship Resources, Nashville, TN 1975.

CHAPTER 2

CAUSES OF HUNGER (PART ONE)

The basic cause of hunger in the world today is poverty. Whether it occurs in the food-deficit nations of the developing world or among low-income groups in the affluent, food-surplus nations, hunger exists because people are poor. According to the World Bank, approximately 800 million people live in such absolute poverty that they cannot provide themselves with even a minimally adequate diet. They live in destitution in crowded urban slums or in neglected rural villages without access to education, health care, or other basic human services. Their housing is as inadequate as their food supply—for some it is only the shade of a tree. They cannot find employment because there are not enough jobs to go around, or because they have no marketable skills nor the means to develop them. Such people are trapped by poverty. Even when "bumper crops" are harvested and storage bins are filled to overflowing, they will not be fed, for food still goes to those who can pay for it. Thus, even doubling food production in the world would not materially change the status of the great majority who are hungry and malnourished today.

How do we account for this extreme inequity between

the rich and the poor? Its roots may be traced to the economic, political, and social systems which have emerged over the last four hundred years.

Colonization

During the sixteenth, seventeenth, and eighteenth centuries the rich nations of the Northern Hemisphere conquered and began to control other territories around the world. These conquered lands became colonies which were exploited to increase the wealth and power of the colonizers. The colonizing countries removed large quantities of gold, silver, and other precious resources which they found in the subjugated lands. They also discovered the tropical climates to be suitable for growing crops that could be sold on the home market, such as tea, coffee, bananas, sugar, and cotton. In time they developed huge export industries which drastically changed the agricultural system of the colonized nations. Food crops for the local population were replaced by the cultivation of export crops, leaving them with an inadequate agriculture to supply their own food needs.

When food for export became the leading industry, the colonies became economically dependent upon the colonizers' markets.

As this pattern continued for several centuries, there was a massive transfer of wealth and power from the colonized countries to the rich nations. Local economies were neglected as political and economic control fell into the hands of foreigners. Today, despite their political independence, many of the former colonies remain trapped in poverty because of their economic dependence on the advanced industrialized nations. President Julius Nyerere of Tanzania made this point at the World Conference on Agrarian Reform and Rural Development in July of 1979:

> Under the economic, political and social systems at present operating, the world's people are divided into two groups; those with access to existing resources — the rich — can afford to invest heavily in the production of greater wealth, so they get richer. The poor have very little to invest; their productivity consequently remains low, and they remain poor. Worse still, the market laws of supply and demand mean that the wealth of the few diverts the world's resources — including the labor of others — from meeting the real but ineffective demand of the poor, into satisfying the luxury desires of the rich. Land and labor are used to cultivate grapes instead of grain; palaces are built instead of houses for the workers and peasants.[1]

An example of the "real but ineffective demand of the poor" Nyerere refers to is described by a Philippine economist:

> The penetration of the [Philippine] countryside by global interests improved agricultural productivity but worsened the problem of social equity. The country is now exporting rice but the quality of life of the people who produce rice has not substantially improved. The surplus in cereal production may merely mean a surplus in terms of demand, and the only

demand that is measured is the demand of those who can pay. The claim of self-sufficiency in rice is false as long as so many of the people are undernourished.[2]

Similarly, India has a current grain surplus of 20 million tons while 48 percent of the rural population live below the official poverty line and cannot afford to buy the grain they need for an adequate diet.

The economic and political systems operating at present are actually widening the gap between the rich and the poor. As Nyerere suggests, despite the investment of rich countries in the developing world, benefits flow to the rich while almost totally bypassing the poor. This is well documented in South and Southeast Asia:

> A most disconcerting paradox of economic development in . . . South and Southeast Asia has been the persistence of acute rural poverty while the rest of the economy records tangible gains. Whichever way poverty is measured, Asia's rural poor have become poorer in most countries in the region, and in some cases the relative size of the class of the rural poor has increased. A variety of indicators such as time-trends in the proportion of the population below the poverty line, in the incidence of malnutrition, in the real income and consumption of the lowest 20 percent of the rural population, in the relative size of the class of agricultural laborers and in rural wage rates all point towards worsening conditions in rural Asia.
>
> Stagnating economic growth is not the blame. Most Asian countries have achieved quite impressive economic growth, both in absolute and per capita terms. . . . Nor can the "population explosion" provide an explanation. There is no evidence whatsoever to suggest that economic growth has been adversely affected by either the initial population density or the rate of demographic expansion. There is just one unavoidable conclusion: growth is the problem. It is not the lack of growth but its very occurrence that is the factor responsible for deteriorating living standards of the rural poor. Growth itself has been impoverishing.[3]

The Impact of Multinational Corporations

Most current economic growth in Third World countries has been spurred by the activity of multinational corporations. These companies, based in advanced industrialized nations, have argued that their presence will bring many benefits to the developing countries. These benefits are supposed to accelerate development through speeding up industrialization, create employment, transfer technology, bring in capital, and generate foreign exchange earnings. But these claims have seldom proved true.

Some development experts say that industrialization of this nature is controlled by and serves the interests of the foreign investor. At the same time, it tends to prevent the host country from establishing its own industries. The Third World economy actually becomes an appendage of the global corporation—the country, a sweatshop of unlimited cheap labor. It is becoming clear to those studying development problems that multinational corporations do not contribute appreciably to employment in Third World countries, and key positions are reserved for foreign managers and technicians.[4]

Very little technology is actually transferred from the industrialized nations as a result of multinational activity in Third World nations. Local workers have minimum access to such technology. They are thus denied opportunity to increase their stock of industrial knowledge and skills. Most technology transferred is done so only in the geographical sense. Control of it still remains with the multinational corporations. They simply transfer the technology to their own representatives in the host country. Since licensor and licensee represent the same corporate interest, they are able to withhold technological information from potential competitors. In the Philippines, for example, 90 percent of the patents are held by foreigners.

Most multinationals create products which are tailored to fit the needs of home markets. These are produced by integrating various partial operations which are scattered in many different countries. The products are then marketed in various countries whether or not they are appropriate for the local population. Some multinational corporations engaged in direct marketing in developing countries have been major contributors to the development of consumer tastes which have a very negative developmental impact. An example of this has occurred in Latin America where peasant farmers sold their meager supply of eggs in order to purchase Coca-Cola while their children suffered from malnutrition.[5]

The economic, political, and social systems presently prevailing have emphasized rapid economic growth. The assumption is that benefits will "trickle down" to the poor. Instead, the present system is predisposed to favor the rich. Tanzanian President Nyerere summarizes what has happened and why most benefits do not reach the poor.

The major benefit of . . . new investment stays where it began — with the man who already has, and in proportion to the wealth which he already has. The poor benefit — or sometimes suffer — from the side effects; or they receive the crumbs left over.

The automatic market tendency to favor the rich is aggravated by the fact that political power also flows naturally to the "haves" of the world — the educated and those persons or societies which have inherited public or private capital. The result is that publicly produced wealth also benefits the

wealthy more than the poor, accrues to the towns more than to the rural areas, and serves the educated rather than those without academic opportunity or ability.[6]

Multinational investment also frequently results in a net outflow of capital from the host country. Repatriated profits from corporate investments are often excessive with nearly a three to one ratio of resource return to the United States.[7]

The Food Export Industry

The food export industry is a particular example of how Third World populations are impoverished by current economic growth. Typical of the effect is that being experienced in the Philippines. One U.S. multinational corporation there has been able to obtain a twenty-five-year contract to lease as much as 17,000 acres of land for only one peso (approximately fourteen cents U.S. currency) per acre for cash crop plantation agriculture. This is part of the government's plan to encourage foreign investment. Using "strong-armed" tactics and intimidation, small farmers have been driven from their lands to make way for the plantations. In some cases the homes and crops of poor tenant farmers have been bulldozed to hasten the conversion of the land to pineapple and banana crops for export. Those who thus become landless flee to urban slums or stay to work at poverty wages as laborers on land that was once their own.[8]

The sugar industry in the Philippines is a similar case. Vast cane fields provide jobs for some 400,000 workers at an average wage of $7.00 per week for thirteen- to fourteen-hour days. Meanwhile corporate profits averaged $3.58 for every $1.00 invested from 1950-70,

$2.00 of which returned to the United States. Multinationals have found that they can save as much as 47 percent of the cost of production by exploiting only the wage differential between American and Filipino workers. An example is that of the Del Monte Corporation, which in 1973 moved its pineapple plantations from Hawaii to the Philippines. The U.S. Congressional Record for November 9, 1973, states:

While Hawaiian plantation workers earn $2.64 an hour, Del Monte pays its Philippine plantation workers 15 cents an hour. Hawaiian cannery workers get paid $2.69 an hour compared to the 20 cents an hour Del Monte pays Philippine workers for the same job.[9]

Cash crops which are produced with extremely low worker wages for export at low prices to developed nations are a form of subsidy from the plantation workers to the ultimate consumers of the products. In addition, the plantation workers act as an "economic shock absorber" for an important part of the world food economy. They may be laid off without benefits when there is over-production, or "retired" without pensions or aid when they become too old or too sick to work.

Poor countries have become even poorer as they have been led to produce only one or two commodities for export. The majority of the non-oil producing countries depend on one, or at most a few, commodities for export income. Prices for primary commodities (raw materials) on the international market are traditionally low, and fluctuate greatly. For example, in less than ten years, the price of raw sugar varied from three cents a pound to about sixty cents per pound.[10] Also, the prices for primary products have not kept pace with those for manufactured goods. From 1950 to 1972 the prices of raw materials increased by only 26 percent while those for manufactured goods increased by 69 percent.

Conclusion

The historical roots of hunger are clearly identified in today's economic, political, and social systems. The inequity we witness in the world has developed over several centuries and will not be quickly or easily changed. Making the prevailing world systems more just will require the adoption of new guiding principles and the political will to make them operable.

[Present] cultural values assert that the purpose of a society is to produce and to consume in the international manner, but by that criterion a rapidly increasing proportion of the world population has no social role. Perhaps as many as two billion people on earth are not needed to produce and they have no money to consume. Why then are they here?
. . . The political and economic system that operates in most of the world denies value to the majority of the world's population. This is the heart of the global human rights problem and it is the reason why the energy to mobilize societies to meet basic needs is lacking. There is no possibility of meeting basic human needs unless the energy of people themselves is released. That can happen only when the development process is guided by a set of values quite different from those which undergird the global shopping center.[11]

The U.S. Presidential Commission on World Hunger describes the importance of political will if such changes are to be implemented.

Human self-interests, human judgments, and human actions all lie at the roots of hunger. Each major cause of hunger could be averted or overcome if the human community were to act cooperatively and decisively. Conversely, the persistence of hunger reflects a lack of sufficient political will

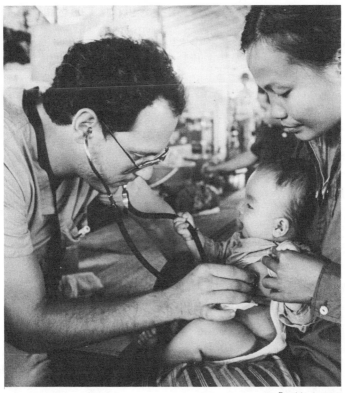

to eliminate its causes. . . . Effective action often will require a degree of political courage which is rare anywhere in the world, as established interests are challenged and hallowed traditions are undone. . . . If hunger is indeed to be overcome, there must be a candid appreciation of its causes, a real willingness to work for the common good of all . . ., and an authentic sharing of economic and political power among and within all nations.[12]

Reflection and Discussion Questions

1. How do you respond to President Julius Nyerere's analysis of why the rich of the world are getting richer and the poor, poorer? Please explain. Record and discuss your own analysis if it is different from Nyerere's.

   _____

   _____

   _____

   _____

2. How many products imported from other countries might you have taken for granted? Have you ever thought about how and where they were produced and by whom? What will you think about such products in the future?

3. If you were living in a developing country how do you think you would feel about growing crops like sugar and coffee for export on land where you once grew food for your family? Record your thoughts.

   _____

   _____

   _____

   _____

   _____

4. "While the United Nations talks of a New Economic Order—one with a more equitable distribution of the world's resources—an entirely different world order is being quietly constructed. Giant corporations, through mergers and expansion into different products and countries, are occupying more of the power structure around us. An assessment of the 100 largest economic powers in the world shows fifty-three to be countries and forty-seven multinational corporations."[13] How do you feel about this observation? Record your feelings and discuss with someone.

_____

_____

_____

_____

5. Should business corporations be responsible to anyone other than boards of directors or (in some cases) stockholders? If so, how could this be done?

6. In what direction do you think Third World nations should develop? Should they follow what other nations have done or determine their own ends and means? If they choose the latter course, what steps may they need to follow?

_____   _____

_____   _____

_____   _____

7. Would some of the causes of hunger discussed in this chapter also apply to hunger in the country where you live? List the ones which apply.

_____   _____

_____   _____

_____   _____

_____   _____

Action Suggestions

1. Make a list of the foods and other products that you use in one week which are produced in another country. Check one product on your list which you believe contributes to global hunger. Find out where it is produced and/or who makes it, what raw materials are used, and any other facts available. Find out as much as you can about the product and report your findings to the group.

_____   _____

_____   _____

_____   _____

_____   _____

2. Select three developing countries and find out what their leading exports are. Are there similarities? Are they "primary" products?

	Country	Products
1.	_____	_____
2.	_____	_____
3.	_____	_____

3. Study a multinational corporation to find out about its overseas operations (such as Castle and Cooke or United Brands). Where have they invested? What do they import from their foreign investment?

Corporation	Where Invested	Imports
_____	_____	_____
		_____
		_____
		_____
_____	_____	_____
		_____
		_____
		_____

Corporation	Where Invested	Imports
_____	_____	_____
		_____
		_____
		_____

4. Before the next group session, develop a list of guiding principles or outline a set of values which you believe could result in a more equitable and just world order. (This could be done by two or three group members working together.) Report to the group at the next session and discuss. Include a discussion of how you would put these principles or values to work in the international order.

Guiding Principles/Values

1. _____

2. _____

3. _____

4. _____

5. _____

6. _____

7. _____

8. _____

Worship Suggestions

The group shares in the following scriptural reflection:

Leader: "For if a brother or sister be naked and desti-
tute, and one of you say, Depart in peace, be
warmed and filled; notwithstanding he give not
those things which are needful to the body; what
profit is your faith unto such?"—James 2:16

Group: With our own needs amply provided for, it's
easy to say to others, "God will provide."

Leader: "You yourselves will succor those that stand in
need of your succor; you will administer of your
substance unto him that standeth in need; and
you will not suffer that the beggar will put up his
petition to you in vain, and turn him out to
perish.

"Perhaps you will say, The man has brought
upon himself his misery; therefore I will stay my
hand, and will not give unto him of my food,
nor impart unto him of my substance, that he
may not suffer, for his punishments are just.

"But I say to you, O man, whosoever does
this, the same hath great cause to repent; and

55

except he repents of that which he has done, he will perish forever, and have no interest in the kingdom of God."—Mosiah 2:28-31

Group: We can no longer consider ourselves virtuous Christians and refuse to respond to the great cry for justice rising from the throats of millions in the hungry world. Justice is not selective: we cannot preach "liberty and justice for all" while we still involve ourselves as individuals, as a church or a nation, in oppressive systems.[14]

Leader: "For behold, are we not all beggars? Do we not all depend upon the same being, even God, for all the substance which we have; for both food and raiment, and for gold, and for silver, and for all the riches which we have of every kind. . . .

"Now, if God, who has created you, on whom you are dependent for your lives, and for all that you have and are, grants to you whatever you ask that is right, in faith, believing that you shall receive, oh then, how had you ought to impart of the substance that you have, one to another?"—Mosiah 2:32, 36

Group: It is frightening, but also exciting. For we, too, in all our riches, experience a kind of hunger. We look for something more, something which transcends the pleasures of the moment. We look for real community, real worth, for something to give ourselves to wholly and completely. That something is the hungry world, and the Lord who wears its face.[15]

Leader: People who give up their own comfort, so that others can be helped, know what heaven is all about. Lord, let us be like these!

Close the session with silent prayer and meditation.

Teacher's Guide

Learning Objectives

At the close of this session participants will be able to
1. name the basic cause of hunger in the world.
2. state approximately how many of the world's population live in absolute poverty.
3. describe the historical process which contributed to the division of the world into rich and poor countries.
4. identify economic, political, or social factors which operate today to continue and/or increase the gap between the rich and the poor.
5. suggest an area in which change must occur if there is to be a more equal distribution of the earth's resources.

Overview of Chapter 2

In Chapter 2 the author describes poverty as the basic cause of hunger. The gap between today's rich and poor nations is traced to the historical process whereby some nations colonized others, and to the ensuing economic and political relationships between these countries. Examples are cited of the economic and political activities which continue to widen the gap between rich and poor (both between and within nations). The world's wealth and power is unequally divided. It is suggested that changing this condition will require the adoption of new guiding principles or values.

Recommended Procedure

1. Ask those who volunteered at the last session to carry out the Chapter 1 "Action Suggestions" to report to the group. If the group decides to start a community food bank (as suggested in number four) this will require group effort and the enlistment of congregational support on a relatively long-term basis. It will be essential for the leader to obtain information from the Second Harvest Network (see p. 34).

2. Review and outline for the group the major points discussed in Chapter 2. Post a large world map on the wall for reference.

3. Discuss the "Reflection and Discussion Questions." Share with one another how the questions relate to your own experience.

4. Enlist volunteers to carry out the "Action Suggestions." (Several people may do the same one.) Ask two or three people to work on Suggestion 4. Help them plan a time when they can get together to work on their task.

5. Ask participants to open their books to the Scriptural Reflection at the end of Chapter 2 and lead them in the responsive reading and worship.

Resources Needed

Large world map (to identify colonized/colonizing countries and other countries referred to in the text)

Pointer to use with the map

Writing utensils

Additional Resources

Films

"How Hunger Happens," Filmstrip No. 2 from "A World Hungry." (See reference in Chapter 1, p. 38.) This would be an effective supplement for either this session or the next. Available from the Audio-Visual Library, the Auditorium, P.O. Box 1059, Independence, Missouri 64051. Rental: $8.00.

"The Politics of Food," Mass Media Ministries, 2116 N. Charles St., Baltimore, MD 21218. Rental: $15.00. Stresses the political aspect of the hunger problem; calls for new priorities.

"International Trade Barriers," Mass Media Ministries. Rental: $12.50. Examines the trade aspects of the hunger problem and the role played by multinational corporations.

"Beyond the Next Harvest," CROP, P.O. Box 968, Elkhart, IN 46515. Presents the world food problem, its causes and cures.

Simulation Game

"Starpower," Simile 11, P.O. Box 1023, La Jolla, CA 92037. $3.00. Includes directions on how to make your own kit. Deals with the unequal distribution of wealth and power. Initially participants have a chance to progress from one level of society to another through trading. However, society soon becomes fixed and the group with the most wealth makes the rules of the game.

Books and Background Papers

"Land and Hunger Abroad," Bread for the World Background Paper No. 45. Bread for the World, 32 Union Square East, New York, NY 10003.

"Land and Hunger in the Philippines," Bread for the World Background Paper No. 55.

"Export Cropping in Central America," Bread for the World Background Paper No. 43.

Dean Freudenberger and Paul Minus, *Christian Responsibilty in a Hungry World* (Nashville, Tennessee: Abingdon Press, 1976).

Piero Gheddo, *Why Is the Third World Poor?* (Maryknoll, New York: Orbis Books, 1973).

Notes

1. Julius Nyerere, "On Rural Development," paper delivered at the World Conference on Agrarian Reform and Rural Development, July 13, 1979.
2. Renato Constantino, *The Nationalist Alternative*, Foundation for Nationalist Studies, Quezon City, Philippines, 1980, p. 50.
3. Ajit K. Ghose, Keith Griffin, "Why the Poor Get Poorer," *Far Eastern Economic Review*, July 13, 1979, p. 50.
4. Renato Constantino, *The Nationalist Alternative*, p. 34.
5. "Multinational Corporations and Global Development," Hunger, No. 24, *Impact*, Washington, D.C., July 1980.
6. Julius Nyerere, "On Rural Development."
7. "Multinational Corporations and Global Development."
8. Simone Mennen, "Bulldozers Against the People," *The Other Side*, March 1981, p. 34.
9. Renato Constantino, *The Nationalist Alternative*, p. 29.

10. "Hunger and Global Security," Bread for the World, February 1981, p. 20.
11. Richard J. Barnet, "Multinationals and Development," cited in *The Challenge of World Hunger*, A Study Guide to the Preliminary Report of the Presidential Commission on World Hunger, Bread for the World, 1979, p. 23A.
12. Presidential Commission on World Hunger, *Overcoming World Hunger, The Challenge Ahead*, March 1980, p. 28.
13. Dexter Tiranti, "Brand New World," *New Internationalist*, Issue No. 85, p. 7.
14. Joanne McPortland, "Not Just Words: A Theological Reflection," "A World Hungry," Teleketics, Franciscan Communications Center, Los Angeles, CA.
15. Ibid.

CHAPTER 3

CAUSES OF HUNGER (PART TWO)

In Part One we discussed some of the historical and systemic causes of hunger in the world. In Part Two we will consider some other causes of hunger which are more recent developments—at least in terms of their magnitude.

The Arms Race

Before the advent of today's strategic weapons, nations traditionally "mobilized" for war. Following armed conflict they "demobilized" and things returned to a normal state of affairs. All that has now changed. Today's weapons preclude preparation for war. With "zero lead time," nations now feel that they must always be prepared against instant attack. This has led to a state of constant and permanent mobilization for war. Nations no longer demobilize. They are engaged in a continual escalation of military preparedness and refinement and sophistication of weapons capability.

Preoccupation with military security has displaced human development as a rightful world priority and looms as an obstacle to meeting worldwide human need.

Shortly after becoming president of the United States, Dwight Eisenhower said, "Every gun that is made, every warship launched, every rocket fired signifies, in the final sense, a theft from those who hunger and are not fed, those who are cold and not clothed." The ever-increasing amount of money that is spent on arms and weapons is money that could otherwise be used to help people work their way out of hunger and poverty.

In 1974, the United States spent $78 billion for defense. In 1975 that figure rose to $85 billion. In 1976, the Ford administration proposed a budget of $96 billion. The 1980 budget earmarked $135.7 billion and the budget for 1981 called for expenditures of $153.7 billion for military defense. Estimates for the 1982 defense budget are around $200 billion. These are staggering

sums, difficult to comprehend. We might break down the
FY 1981 budget as follows:

Chart F: U.S. Military Spending in the 1981 Budget[1]
$153,700,000,000 for the year, which equals
$421,095,616 per day which equals
$17,545,650 per hour, or
$292,427.50 per minute.

The budget for fiscal year 1981 called for the spending of
$9.5 billion on foreign affairs and only part of that was for
development purposes.

In 1979, the nations of the world spent almost $450
billion on arms and weapons while official development
aid amounted to *less than 5 percent* of this figure, or
roughly $22 billion. Chart G indicates what some transfer
from military spending to development efforts might
mean.

Chart G: Transfer of Military Spending[2]

1. The military expenditure of only half a day (approximately $616.5 million) would suffice to
   finance the whole malaria eradication program of
   the World Health Organization, and less would be
   needed to conquer river-blindness (onchocerchi-
   asis), which is still the scourge of millions.
2. A modern tank costs about one million dollars; that
   amount could improve storage facilities for 100,000
   tons of rice and thus save 4000 tons or more an-
   nually. One person can live on just over a pound of

---

rice a day. The same sum of money could provide 1000 classrooms for 30,000 children.

3. For the price of one jet fighter ($20 million) about 40,000 village pharmacies could be set up.

4. One-half of one percent of one year's world military expenditure (approximately $2¼ billion) would pay for all the farm equipment needed to increase food production and approach self-sufficiency in food-deficit low-income countries by 1990.

Abusing the Earth/Wasting the Resources

The desert is spreading in Africa and in North America. The rivers and the air are being polluted with chemicals which are killing the fish and changing the climate in ways unknown to us. Every year more and more fertile topsoil is lost through erosion and the lack ot flood control. Cattle and sheep overgraze the land, and too many trees are cut down in many diverse geographical areas. Each of these factors also contribute to hunger in the world.

Population Growth

Rapid population growth is contributing to the strain on the world's food producing systems. There is a commonly held assumption that overpopulation *causes* hunger and poverty. However, experts in this area are beginning to realize that the opposite may very well be the case, namely, that *poverty causes overpopulation*. The U.S. Presidential Commission on World Hunger had this to report:

Where hunger and poverty prevail, the population growth rate is more likely to increase than to decrease. Under

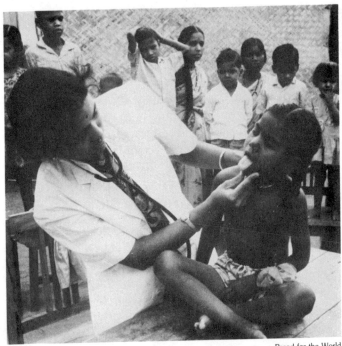

Bread for the World

inequitable social and economic conditions, a poor couple's desire for many children is a response to high infant mortality, the need for extra hands to help earn the family's daily bread and the hope of support in old age. The key to reducing family size is to improve the social conditions.[3]

The Affluence Explosion

The increasing demands of rising affluence in the industrialized nations are other factors contributing to world hunger. Consumption patterns of the affluent populations in industrialized countries have diverted food

Bread for the World

and other resources from the hungry poor. As these
societies have become wealthier, their consumption of
animal products has increased. This means that more of
the basic foodstuffs such as grains, legumes, and fish that
could feed humans directly are instead fed to animals.
The net effect of this trend is that rich nations consume far
more food per capita than poor ones. Each person in the
United States consumes, on the average, the equivalent
of 1,850 pounds of grain per year, compared with 400
pounds in the poor countries. While the population of the
United States represents 6 percent of the world's population, we use 34 percent of the earth's resources. Energy

67

is another example. Air-conditioners in the United States alone consume as much energy as does the entire nation of China, with its 800 plus million people.

Dr. A. H. Borma, former Director General of the U.N. Food and Agriculture Organization, compared food consumption in the rich nations with that of populations in the poor countries: "The developed world feeds more cereals to its livestock than are consumed as food by all the vast populations of the developing countries together."[4] In 1972, the Soviet Union bought 19 million tons of grain in the United States, suddenly erasing the U.S. surplus of grain. Those purchases were based on a Soviet decision to feed their livestock and keep meat flowing to Soviet tables, despite poor harvests. Grain prices soared and additional millions went hungry. The hungry poor were priced out of the grain markets, where the highest bidder gets the commodities.

Wrong Priorities

In recent years, a number of different groups that have studied the problems of hunger and malnutrition have suggested that another major cause of hunger in the world is the lack of priority given to its elimination by the nations of the world. The U.S. Presidential Commission on World Hunger concluded the following:

The Commission concludes that neither the developing countries, the developed nations nor international institutions have given sufficient priority to ending hunger and malnutrition by addressing its causes. In the developing countries, domestic political problems, national security questions, and industrial development generally have attracted more attention and resources than alleviating poverty or investing in agriculture. In fact, few nations have even made these latter concerns top developmental priorities. The

development of remote, backward rural areas has had little political or psychological appeal to civilian or military rulers bent on maintaining their control and modernizing their societies along sophisticated technological and industrial lines. Adopting the priorities of the industrialized world, many Third World leaders have modernized their armies and parts of their cities at the expense of their agriculture, health care and education.[5]

Nor are the developed countries committed to the elimination of hunger.

The United States and other developed nations, too, have placed a very low priority on alleviating world hunger. Since World War II, the industrialized countries have been preoccupied with East-West tensions and sustaining domestic economic growth. These primary concerns have largely determined both the nature and extent of the West's involvement with the developing world....The hard reality is that the overwhelming majority of the world's hungry people live in countries which have been of limited significance to world grain markets and to Western geopolitical concerns.[6]

What the commission is suggesting is that the elimination of hunger is a question of political *will*.

Conclusion

We have the capability of eliminating hunger in the world if we make it a priority. We can—we just haven't. The governments of the world have verbalized this goal, but have not really committed themselves to working for it. Our earlier discussion about military spending is a good example of this. The United States spends more money on military purposes *in one day* than is spent *in an entire year* by the U.N. World Food Program. Every sixteen hours, the U.S. Defense Department spends more than the World Health Organization and the Food and Agriculture Organization spend in one year. The United States allocates .27 percent—just over one-fourth of 1 percent—of its entire gross national product for development assistance in a year. The U.S. government will not make the elimination of hunger a priority unless its citizens demand such a priority. Is the elimination of hunger a priority for us as a people? The U.S. Presidential Commission on World Hunger offers this challenge:

In the end, the issue of ending world hunger comes down to a question of political choice—a factor that is no more predictable than the weather, but far more susceptible to human control. The quantities of food and money needed to wipe out hunger are remarkably small in relation to available global resources. The necessary human ingenuity also abounds in all nations of the world, although that quality is too often harnessed to different and often conflicting goals. The Commission agrees with other studies that if the appropriate political choices are made, the world can overcome the worst aspects of hunger and malnutrition by the year 2000. This end can be accomplished through the alleviation of malnutrition in the world of today, in tandem with more fundamental efforts to build a future world in which hunger will be unknown.[7]

Reflection and Discussion Questions

1. Do you believe that the people of the United States are willing to make the elimination of hunger a priority? An assessment of expenditures for various items of personal consumption tells us something about priorities in the United States.

Chart H: U.S. Development Assistance Compared to Expenditures for Selected Items of Personal Consumption 1978[8]
($ billion)

Alcoholic Beverages	30.9
Tobacco Products	17.9
Household Cleaning Supplies	16.4
Toys and Sport Supplies	11.7
Foreign Travel and Tourist Expenditures Abroad	11.6
Jewelry and Watches	9.3
Admission to Spectator Amusements	7.4
Barber Shops and Beauty Parlors	5.9
Official Development Assistance	5.7
Brokerage Charges and Investment Counseling	5.5

(Source: Department of Commerce)

Share and discuss your feelings about these expenditures.

Do you believe that other Western nations of the world want to make elimination of hunger their priority? Why do you believe this?

2. What do you think of the statement "poverty causes overpopulation"? At the U.N. Population Conference in Bucharest representatives of the participating countries said, "The hungry nations have a right to reduce their population growth rates the same way that the United States and other industrialized nations have reduced theirs: within the context of social and economic gains." Discuss with the group what this means to you.

3. List some ways other than those mentioned in which waste contributes to hunger. Make a second list of what you can do to stop this.

How Waste Contributes   How I Can Stop This

_____   _____

_____   _____

_____   _____

_____   _____

_____   _____

4. How do you react to the following statement?

Nothing is more grimly characteristic of the age than the fact that the finest minds are not being directed to the biggest problems. Brains are being honed and mobilized for purposes of confrontation and destruction. No comparable mobilization of human intellect and conscience is occurring on the level of humanity's greatest needs.[9]

a. What would you list as humanity's greatest needs?

_____   _____

_____   _____

_____   _____

_____   _____

b. How would you redirect the "mobilization of human intellect and conscience" to address these needs? Record your thoughts.

_____

_____

_____

_____

5. How would you define national security?

_____

_____

_____

_____

6. List the major causes of hunger as you now understand them.

_____   _____

_____   _____

_____   _____

_____   _____

_____   _____

Worship Suggestions

Ask one person to read the following excerpt:

The reality of hunger in our world is so immense that many people throw up their arms in frustration and don't even try to respond. "I can't make a difference in any real way, so what's the use of trying" is their typical comment. In some contexts, that comment seems to make sense. The actions of one person against so large a problem do seem insignificant.

For Christians, such despair is out of order. We have in God's Kingdom the promise of peace and justice to encourage, strengthen and sustain us. The disciples learned at the feeding of the 5,000 and we also know that when we place our efforts in the Lord's hands, they will be enough. For Christians not to hope and not to act in the face of hunger is despair — and despair is unbelief.

Our actions on behalf of the hungry need not be immediately successful to have meaning. We believe that the future is with God's Kingdom. No efforts consistent with this hope are wasted. They are signs of the Kingdom and through them God does his work.[10]

Another person reads the following scripture:

Yea, saith the Lord, I desire many evangelists of love to preach the gospel of love, not only in word but also in deed.... You are admonished that you be not unduly concerned because you are few in number as compared with the world. That is not your concern, but be concerned only that your righteousness shall be very great. For a few righteous men can accomplish very much, and a little leaven leaveneth a great lump.[11]

Sing together the first verse of Hymn No. 451, *Hymns of the Saints:*

"O Church of God, arise and take thy lamp of love,

The light that never dies on earth, in heaven above!

With wisdom and with truth keep quick and straight the flame,

The light of love and youth, to save a world of shame."

Use the following scripture as a closing prayer:

And they shall beat their swords into ploughshares, and their spears into pruning hooks; nation shall not lift up a sword against nation, neither shall they learn war anymore.

But they shall sit every man under his vine and under his fig tree; and none shall make them afraid; for the mouth of the Lord of hosts hath spoken it. — Micah 4:3, 4

Teacher's Guide

Learning Objectives

At the close of this session participants will be able to

1. describe the current state of military preparedness in the world as compared to that of pre-World War II.
2. state the approximate amount of money being spent worldwide on arms and weapons.
3. describe the current status of human development as a world priority.
4. explain the relationship of population growth to hunger.
5. list the major causes of hunger.

Overview of Chapter 3

Chapter 3 contains a description of the change that today's weapons of war have wrought upon the world. The perceived need for all nations to be armed against instant attack has led to a preoccupation with military preparedness. This condition is presented as a major cause of poverty and hunger. Other causes are abuse and waste of the earth's resources, hunger-spawned population growth, rising affluence in the developed nations, and the failure of world societies to treat the elimination of

hunger as a priority. Generation of the human will to end
hunger is suggested as a primary challenge.

Recommended Procedure

1. Ask those who volunteered to carry out the "Action
   Suggestions" in Chapter 2 to report to the group. Be
   sure to allow adequate time to hear the group who
   worked on Suggestion 4. (They may want to meet
   again before finalizing and presenting their report. If
   so, make plans for them to report later.)
2. Review with the entire group the key points in
   Chapter 3, and discuss the questions at the end of
   the chapter. You may want to ask two or three
   people to work on Question 4 together during the
   week and report at the next session.
3. Enlist two people to lead the group in the closing
   worship as suggested. Pass out hymnals if you wish
   to sing more than the first verse of Hymn No. 451,
   Hymns of the Saints.

Resources Needed

An overhead projector (to facilitate discussion of
Chart H)
Hymnals
Texts for reference
Writing utensils

Additional Resources

Films

"How Hunger Happens," Filmstrip No. 2 from "A

World Hungry." (If not used for Chapter 2 [See reference in Chapter 1, p. 38.])

Books

Arthur Simon, *Bread for the World*, ch. 3, 5, 12.
Lester Brown, *The Twenty-Ninth Day*, Norton Press, New York, 1978.

Notes

1. Calculated by Anthony Cernera, BFW Educational Fund Staff, July 1980.
2. Willy Brandt, *North-South: A Program for Survival*, MIT Press, 1980, p. 14.
3. U.S. Presidential Commission on World Hunger, *Overcoming World Hunger: The Challenge Ahead*, 1980, p. 25.
4. *When I Was Hungry, A Hunger Course for High School Students*, Bread for the World Educational Fund, New York, NY, 1980, p. 24.
5. U.S. Presidential Commission on World Hunger, p. 43.
6. Ibid., p. 45.
7. Ibid.
8. U.S. International Development Cooperation Agency, *Congressional Presentation*, Fiscal Year 1981, p. 22.
9. Norman Cousins, *Saturday Review World*, December 14, 1974, p. 5.
10. *Leaven*, Bread for the World Covenant Church Quarterly, Fall, 1980, p. 3.
11. Percy E. Farrow, *God's Eternal Design*, Herald Publishing House, Independence, MO, 1980, p. 238.

CHAPTER 4

SCRIPTURAL PERSPECTIVES ON HUNGER

Photo by John Cackler

As we seek to eliminate the causes of hunger, we should be guided by the vision of a better way. Our work cannot be just to eliminate something; it must be to substitute something better. As Christians we want the scriptures to instruct our responses to hunger. We rely upon scriptural perspectives to help us envision a way of life that will provide for everyone's need.

The Value of Human Life

Central to the Christian gospel is the affirmation of the great worth of every human life. The gospel of John records, "God so loved the world that he gave his Only Begotten Son, that whosoever believeth on him should not perish; but have everlasting life" (John 3:16). In giving up his life for our sakes, Jesus proclaimed human life of infinite value and the object of his divine love. Other scriptures affirm the worth as well as the dignity of human life. A contemporary scripture states, "Remember, the worth of souls is great in the sight of God; for behold the Lord your Redeemer suffered death in the flesh; wherefore he suffered the pain of all men, that all men might repent and come unto him" (Doctrine and Covenants 16:3c). The Psalmist declared, "What is man, that thou art mindful of him? And the son of man, that thou visitest him? For thou hast made him a little lower than the angels, and hast crowned him with glory and honor" (Psalm 8:4). In spite of scriptural assurance of the great worth of human life, millions of people are being treated as if their lives are of very little value. Every life lost because of hunger is an instance of human life devalued.

In the creation story we are told, "And I, God, created man in mine own image, in the image of mine Only Begotten created I him; male and female created I them" (Genesis 1:29). The explanation that humans are created in the likeness of God suggests a personhood that goes beyond the physical and includes a spiritual likeness. The scriptures state: "For I, the Lord God, created all things of which I have spoken, spiritually, before they were naturally upon the face of the earth" (Genesis 2:5) and "Man was also in the beginning with God...for man is spirit" (Doctrine and Covenants 90:5a, d). If humans are created in the divine likeness, physically and spiritually, we cannot expect human fulfillment to be found in a way of life that is foreign to God. And God's way was made very clear to us in the life of Jesus.

Love and Justice

The gospel outlines a way of life that will bring us joy and fulfillment. The life of Christ epitomizes ultimate human life. It reveals a way to wholeness and self-realization. The center of that revelation is unconditional, self-sacrificing love. In two of his most dramatic stories—the parables of the prodigal son and the good Samaritan—Christ taught his followers that they were to love without judgment or conditional requirements, and that love was *authentic* as it was expressed in action.

Christ embodied all that had been taught God's people from the beginning about how they were to live in relationship with one another. In an unfolding revelation of God's will through the prophets, the Israelites were called to the recognition that God had freed them from oppression and injustice in Egypt, and that to be faithful to God, they must similarly free the oppressed and do justice to others. God's definition of their task in the world was "to do justly, and to love mercy, and to walk humbly with . . . God" (Micah 6:8). When the people forgot about this task and feigned worship and fasting while living in wickedness, Isaiah told them again that the Lord expected more than words and rituals, he expected acts of justice and mercy:

Is not this the fast that I have chosen? to loose the bands of wickedness, to undo the heavy burdens, and to let the

oppressed go free, and that ye break every yoke? Is it not to deal thy bread to the hungry, and that thou bring the poor that are cast out to thy house? when thou seest the naked, that thou cover him?

—Isaiah 58:6, 7

He describes a true fast, the fast he expects, as a fast from wickedness. He goes on to explain that when we do righteousness and justice—when we share our bread with the hungry and care for the homeless poor—the Lord will hear our prayers and we shall be like a "watered garden" (Isaiah 58:11).

Amos, a poor shepherd, called the people back to justice when Israel was at the height of her economic and political power. He announced the punishment of God on the people because, again, they pretended to worship God while their lives were filled with wickedness. The injustice in which the rich were engaging completely negated the value of their worship.

"[The Lord says] I hate your religious festivals; I cannot stand them! When you bring me burnt offerings and grain offerings, I will not accept them; I will not accept the animals you have fattened to bring me as offerings. Stop your noisy songs; I do not want to listen to your harps. Instead, let justice flow like a stream, and righteousness like a river that never goes dry."

—Amos 5:21-24 (TEV)

When there is no justice, life is barren and worship of God is a sham.

Just as the prophets of Israel taught the people that actions were the measure of their faith, King Benjamin told the people of ancient America that if they really believed in God they would do according to his word. He proclaimed that God expects people to care for the needy and exposed one of the excuses we use when we withhold our help.

You yourselves will succor those that stand in need of your succor; you will administer of your substance to him that stands in need; and you will not suffer that the beggar will put up his petition to you in vain, and turn him out to perish.

Perhaps you will say, The man has brought upon himself his misery; therefore I will stay my hand, and will not give to him of my food, nor impart to him of my substance, that he may not suffer, for his punishments are just.

But I say unto you, O man, whoever does this, the same has great cause to repent; and except he repents of that which he has done, he will perish forever, and hath no interest in the kingdom of God.

For behold, are we not all beggars? Do we not all depend upon the same being, even God, for all the substance which we have; for both food, and raiment, and for gold, and for silver, and for all the riches which we have of every kind. . . .

Now, if God, who has created you, on whom you are dependent for your lives and for all that ye have and are, grants to you whatever you ask that is right, in faith, believing that you shall receive, oh, then, how had you ought to impart of the substance that you have, one to another?

And if you judge the man who puts up his petition to you for your substance, that he perish not, and condemn him, how much more just will be your condemnation, for withholding your substance, which does not belong to you, but to God, to whom also, your life belongs.

—Mosiah 2:28-37

Jesus' Ministry: The Work of Justice

Early in his public ministry Jesus defined his own mission in terms of service to the poor, the outcasts, and the downtrodden. In the synagogue he read from Isaiah the words which described his ministry:

"The Spirit of the Lord is upon me, because he has chosen me to bring good news to the poor. He has sent me to proclaim liberty to the captives and recovery of sight to the blind, to set free the oppressed and announce that the time has come when the Lord will save his people."—Luke 4:18-19 (TEV)

Bread for the World

The love Christ taught and lived was a *radical* love. He commanded his disciples to, "love one another, as I have loved you" (John 15:12). He advocated not only loving those of the fellowship, but added, "Love your enemies; bless them that curse you" (Matthew 5:46). He explained that this was the way to be "children of your Father who is in heaven," who, "maketh his sun to rise on the evil and on the good" (Matthew 5:47).

He went on to emphasize, just as the prophets had to Israel, that such love was to be expressed in deed, not just word. In Matthew 25, Jesus described eternal life as a reward contingent upon whether or not we care for the needy. In this scripture Jesus identified himself with those who are in need and thus indicated their importance to him.

Then shall he say also unto them on the left hand, Depart from me, ye cursed, into everlasting fire, prepared for the devil and his angels.

For I was an hungered, and ye gave me no meat; I was thirsty, and ye gave me no drink;

I was a stranger, and ye took me not in; naked, and ye clothed me not; sick, and in prison, and ye visited me not.

Then shall they also answer him, saying, Lord, when saw we thee an hungered, or athirst, or a stranger, or naked, or sick, or in prison, and did not minister unto thee?

Then shall he answer them, saying, Verily I say unto you, Inasmuch as ye did it not to one of the least of these my brethren, ye did it not unto me.

And these shall go away into everlasting punishment; but the righteous into life eternal. — Matthew 25:42-47

When we refuse to help the needy we refuse our Lord. Christ represents himself to us in a special way in the hungry, the naked, the sick, and the prisoner. He is among us in the outcasts and oppressed of our age. Their cry for justice is his cry for justice. And when we respond we find that we are filled, the poor go away rejoicing, and the kingdom comes nearer.

Paul's writing and other material in the New Testament give us insights into the concern for the poor and hungry in the early church. One of the characteristics of this new community was its care for those in need. True to the ways of their Lord, the early church people shared their resources in such a way that there were no poor among them (Acts 4:34).

Speaking of Jesus, Paul reminded us that "though he was rich, yet for your sakes he became poor, that ye through his poverty might be rich" (II Corinthians 8:9). Jesus is the poor one among us. He gave up all, laid down his life that we might live, and in so doing, took it up again. We, too, are promised that "whosoever will save his life, must be willing to lose it for my sake; and whosoever will be willing to lose his life for my sake, the same shall save it" (Luke 9:24).

Conclusion

Jesus, who valued human life so highly that he gave up his own, calls us also to recognize the worth of persons and spend our lives for the sake of others. He demonstrated that this kind of love triumphs over all. Imbued with that love, we labor in a hungry world, knowing that our efforts to end hunger will be multiplied by his power. Through caring for our needy brothers and sisters, we may help to create God's kingdom.

Reflection and Discussion Questions

1. List some ways in which human life is demeaned in today's world.

_____   _____

_____   _____

_____   _____

2. What can you do to promote human dignity?

_____

_____

_____

_____

3. On what occasions have you attached *conditions* to your love and concern for others? What were they?

_____

_____

_____

_____

How might you have withheld help from someone in need because you felt "the man has brought upon himself his misery"? (See Mosiah 2:30.) Discuss.

4. If justice were to flow like a stream, and righteousness like a river (Amos 5:24) in today's world, what kinds of changes would you expect? Record your thoughts.

_____

_____

_____

_____

5. Is there a difference between charity and justice? Please explain.

_____

_____

_____

_____

Action Suggestions

1. Plan a "Third World Visit" for the families in your congregation. Invite a guest who has lived and worked in a developing country to speak to the group about life in that country, including a description of food, clothing, shelter, education, health care, how human life is regarded, and what Christians are doing in that country. Prepare a meal for the group that would be typical in the average home in that country. Discuss similarities between life in that country and life in your own.

2. If you have children in your family (or this could be done with church school class) help them put together a photo montage of children throughout the world. Explore with them the differences between growing up in your country and a country in Asia, Africa, or Latin America.

3. Pray at mealtime for those who suffer from hunger and poverty.

Worship Suggestions

Scripture: "Therefore, all things whatsoever ye would that men should do to you, do ye even so to them; for this is the law and the prophets."—Matthew 7:21

The Theme in Parable

A story is told about a village located on a small island in the South Pacific. For many years the village fishing duties belonged to one family, who passed on the skill from generation to generation. This family took great pride in providing fish for the entire village. In time, however, the village grew to a point where this one family could not provide enough fish for everyone. At first, the village was requested to eat less fish. Then the fishing family worked longer each day to try and catch more fish. Finally, they decided to look for another way to catch fish. After much experimentation, they eventually devised a net to be thrown out into the water which would scoop up more fish than either spearfishing or fishing lines. There was only one problem: the family could not handle the large nets by themselves.

One day, the family sat down with the tribal elders to discuss the problem. After much exploration, there appeared to be only one solution: others from the village would have to learn how to fish. So the family would become teachers as well as fishers.

Many months passed, with more and more people learning how to throw out the nets and draw them back in again. The village once again prospered with enough fish for everyone. But far more importantly, more villagers were engaged in providing food for themselves and

Office of Graphic Arts/Jack Garnier

others. Cooperation and mutual support accomplished what otherwise could not be done.

Scriptural Meditation

Give, and it shall be given unto you; good measure, pressed down, and shaken together, and running over, shall men give into your bosom. For with the same measure that ye mete withal, it shall be measured to you again. — Luke 6:38

Prayer Thought: We pray for openness of mind and willingness of heart to accept God's word as addressed to us, and to practice it in all areas of our lives.

Teacher's Guide

Learning Objectives

At the close of this session students will be able to

1. list some scriptures that proclaim the value of human life.
2. explain how hunger is an affront to human dignity.
3. cite a biblical example of God's displeasure with those who oppressed the poor and lived in wickedness while pretending to worship him.
4. relate scriptural instruction concerning doing justice and helping the needy to the actual life situations of today's world.
5. define the basis for Christian hope in the face of present realities in the world.

Overview of Chapter 4

In Chapter 4 scriptures are quoted that form the basis for the affirmation that every human life is of great worth. In spite of this Christian view of life, millions of people are being treated as if their lives are of very little value. The life of Christ demonstrates how we are meant to live in relationship to one another. When we act justly and care for others as he did we find fulfillment, joy, and the promise of God's kingdom in our midst.

Recommended Procedure

1. Ask volunteers who worked on Question 4 of Chapter 3 to share with the group.
2. Review the content of Chapter 4. Discuss the questions at the end of the chapter, encouraging participants to share their feelings and personal experiences.
3. If there is time, ask the students to choose the scripture passage they liked best and rewrite it in the form of a story. Caution them to be careful to keep

the main point. Have them read their stories to one another.

4. Discuss "Action Suggestion 1" with the group, and make plans to sponsor this activity in your congregation. Ask for volunteers to chair committees to engage the guest speaker, plan the food, lead the discussion, and make the other necessary arrangements. Evaluate this activity as a group following the Third World Visit.

5. Request students who may have young children at home, or who teach a church school class to try "Action Suggestion 2." Ask all participants to do "Suggestion 3."

6. Enlist someone ahead of time to share the Theme in Parable story, as well as the scriptural meditation for the worship. Close the session with the worship as suggested.

Resources Needed

A list of possible speakers for the Third World Visit
Magazines, newspapers, scissors, glue, writing utensils

Additional Resources

Books

John Haughey, *The Faith That Does Justice*, Paulist Press, New York, 1977. Especially Chapter One.

Ronald Sider, *Rich Christians in an Age of Hunger:* A Biblical Study, Intervarsity Press, Downers Grove, IL, 1977.

CHAPTER 5

CORPORATE RESPONSES TO HUNGER

Combating the causes of world hunger requires institutional involvement. Hunger is so widespread and the causes so complex that any effective effort to eliminate it should include the commitment of corporate and governmental bodies. Organizations which we have helped to build, and which we now help to sustain, must be prepared and willing to accept moral and economic responsibility for helping the poor and hungry.

The Church and Hunger

Since its beginning, the Restoration church has been concerned with the poor and needy. As early as 1831 the church was told, "Thou wilt remember the poor, and consecrate of thy properties for their support" (Doctrine and Covenants 42:8b). The concept of stewardship has always been a basic tenet of the church. It challenges members to develop and multiply their gifts and spend them for kingdom-building purposes. Through wise stewardship a surplus of resources is generated, which then is shared with those in need "from time to time, that every [one] who has need may be amply supplied, and receive according to his wants" (Doctrine and Covenants 42:10a). Every person is a steward, "for it is expedient that I, the Lord, should make every [one] accountable, as stewards over earthly blessings, which I have made and prepared for my creatures" (Doctrine and Covenants 101:2c). These blessings are to be used "in the manner designed of God" (Doctrine and Covenants 128:8c).

The Restoration concept of stewardship is more than a scriptural foundation for charity. It is a way of life that recognizes the earth as the home of the whole human family, to be shared equitably according to the *needs and just wants of all*. The concept of stewardship acknowledges the capability, dignity, and promise of every person as a creature possessed of gifts, with the freedom and ability to choose how they will be used. "All are called according to the gifts of God unto them" and invited to "labor together with God for the accomplishment of the work intrusted to all" (Doctrine and Covenants 119:8b).

Church members have generously supported the Oblation fund as a means of giving to those in need. Many also support charitable organizations of all kinds. Other groups of Saints have incorporated several independent agencies dedicated to alleviating poverty and hunger in Third World countries. These efforts have been significant, both in terms of individual stewardship and the effect in the lives of those in need.

World Hunger Program

Since the world food shortages of the early 1970s, and with the continued increase in the number of hungry people in the world, there has been a growing interest in

establishing a World Church program which would address global hunger. At the 1978 World Conference such a program was begun. The church adopted the World Hunger Resolution (GCR 1148), which committed the church to a program of corporate action to alleviate world hunger. The three primary goals of the program are as follows:

1. **To engage the membership of the church in a corporate response to world hunger**
2. **To emphasize, in our worship services, concern for hunger and poverty in the world**
3. **To develop ministries based on the repression of unnecessary wants**

The program was officially introduced on November 25, 1979, as a continuing process involving members in the following: (a) the contribution of funds to a world hunger fund, (b) participation in a church-wide program of hunger education, (c) promotion through personal citizenship and formulation of government policies that address the basic causes of hunger, and (d) conversion to a simpler and less consumptive life-style.

The World Hunger Fund is a special element of the Oblation fund. Contributions are received through duplex offering envelopes, which carry the Oblation World Hunger (OWH) notation. The fund is being used for the following basic purposes:

1. **Support of self-help programs of comprehensive community development, including health, education, and agriculture among impoverished peoples, "giving consideration . . . to our brothers and sisters" (quoted from GCR 1148)**
2. **Support of agencies and programs which provide hunger education, and which seek public policy that advocates the cause of the hungry**
3. **Training of indigenous leaders who will be able to identify the needs of hungry people and develop local resources that will relieve hunger**
4. **Encouragement of church members to take responsibility for changing economic and political structures which spawn hunger.**

Outreach International

Shortly after the introduction of the World Hunger Program, church officials established a foundation to support comprehensive programs of human resources development. This foundation, known as Outreach International, was incorporated in April, 1979. Outreach International

Nutrition Center   Office of Graphic Arts/ Barrie Smith

was commissioned to give appropriate attention to the needs of the poor and disadvantaged of the world. Previously incorporated, independent, church-related organizations engaged in health, agricultural, and educational projects were encouraged to affiliate with Outreach International to obtain the benefits of a united financial appeal, as well as enriched communication and understanding of mutual concerns.[1]

In two years the World Hunger Program and Outreach International have coordinated efforts to fund comprehensive human development projects in sixteen different nations. Contributions to the World Hunger Fund have been disbursed by the World Hunger Committee in consultation with the stipulations of the World Hunger Resolution. To qualify for funding projects must meet the following requirements:

1. Significantly involve local input in decision-making, implementation, leadership, and accountability.
2. Support and facilitate the appropriate technology within the capabilities of the local people (self-development).
3. Share concern for the whole person in the whole community (agriculture, economics, land, education, physical and spiritual health, etc.).
4. Offer a reasonable hope of being continued by the local people when the project is completed (i.e., self-supporting).
5. Attempt to help resolve the global concern of world hunger.[2]

The projects funded to date have included improving agricultural methods and increasing production, improving rural storage and marketing facilities, making improved seeds and fertilizer available, building irrigation systems, supplying potable water, establishing nutrition education programs for mothers and supplemental child feeding programs for children, improving backyard

Office of Graphic Arts/Jack Garnier

gardening, introducing animal and poultry production, providing vocational training, organizing farmers' co-operatives, and helping farmers to become landowners. All projects are developed with the leadership of local persons and with the use of locally developed technologies and resources. A constant emphasis is to advance long-term social change that may prevent problems from recurring. Outreach has consistently promoted development which draws people into productive participation in the economic, political, and social life of their communities.

Public Policy Advocacy

Another part of the hunger program of the church is the encouragement of members toward increasingly responsible citizenship. The underlying causes of hunger, perpetuated by unjust economic and political structures, must be addressed through the political process. Without the influence and resources that governments alone can command, hunger will continue to affect millions of people in the world.

Most people feel helpless about becoming involved in the politics of hunger. Many feel that the government is so large, complex, and resistant to change, that the efforts of ordinary citizens could not make much difference. Some persons also believe that powerful vested interests have taken control of government. Thus, it seems hopeless to attempt to change policies that benefit some and deprive others. Still others feel that the work of the church and its members is to share a spiritual view of life. In their opinion, involvement with the political and economic structures of society is outside the domain of the church and would mean forsaking the church's primary task.

It is true that governments are large and complex, but in democracies like the United States, Great Britain, Canada, and Australia, they are created and empowered by the citizens of the nation. Government is accountable to its citizens. They are the ones who finance and commission it to function on their behalf.

In the gospel of Mark we read that Jesus' disciples went through the cornfields on the Sabbath day and, because they were hungry, they began "to pluck the ears of corn" (Mark 2:21). The Pharisees criticized Jesus for allowing them to do this unlawful thing. Jesus' response is instructive for us. He replied: "The Sabbath was made for man, and not man for the Sabbath" (Mark 2:25). This is also true of government—it was created to serve the people; it should not be served for its sake. If the latter should happen to us, it is by default—and it may happen as persons neglect their citizenship and cease to participate responsibly in all aspects of the political process. Special interest groups become powerful and displace our own power as we neglect to be active citizen participants in government ourselves. The attitude that average citizens can do nothing will help to make it so.

The separation of church and state has always prevailed in the United States as essential to the freedom its citizens enjoy. Individuals may choose their faith or nonfaith according to the dictates of personal conscience. In this manner citizens are assured that human government will not prescribe rules of worship or control the individual conscience. While this does mean that religion will not impose a faith bias upon all people, it does not mean that those people who live by their faith are to be nonparticipants in the functions of government. Every person has the freedom and responsibility to live according to personal beliefs as long as this does not infringe upon the rights and liberties of others. To the extent that persons live as full participants in society, truly representative governments will exist and majority rule will be just. If Christians withhold their participation and influence because they feel religion must not tamper with government, truly representative governments cannot exist. Churches are as much a part of the society as multinational corporations or labor groups or educational institutions. All of the latter are active, persistent, and well-represented participants in the political process. Christians share that kind of responsibility—not for the sake of prescribing for others, but so that *government for the people* shall also be the *government of* and *by the people*. Unless their voices are heard along with all the others, the composite will be distorted and not truly representative.

God valued the agency of humans so highly that he risked losing us and ransomed the divine Life to save us. We may, in return, use God's gifts and blessings, including our citizenship, to help save others. Christians who forfeit by default their right of voice and vote in the political process are giving up one of the most significant ways of helping the poor and hungry of this world.

Public Advocacy Organizations

In a statement by the U.S. Presidential Commission on World Hunger some areas are identified in which con-

cerned church members might begin to focus their efforts.
The commission stated:

**There are compelling moral, economic and national
security reasons for the United States government to make
the elimination of hunger the central focus of its relations
with the developing world. However, neither current U.S.
policies nor prevailing public attitudes demonstrate an accurate understanding of the problems' scope, urgency, or
relevance to America's own national well-being.**

**What is needed to assure that the United States plays its
proper major role in the worldwide campaign against hunger
is a major reordering of national priorities. Additional resources must be mobilized, public understanding and support
must be marshalled, and the government must organize itself
in ways that will enhance the U.S. ability to address this
critical issue.**[3]

There are several Christian groups in the United States
who have already begun to work toward the goals mentioned by the commission. One of these is Bread for the
World. A Christian citizens' movement, Bread for the
World seeks legislative policies that address the basic
causes of hunger. It seeks to reorder priorities, increase
public understanding of the hunger problem's scope and
urgency, and help mobilize support to combat hunger.

Bread for the World began with a small group of Christians from several different churches who met in New
York in October 1972 to share their concerns about world
hunger and poverty. Members of the group felt that
Christians should help to shape public policy relating to
hunger. They concluded that the best way to enable this
would be to organize a nucleus of Christians in every
United States Congressional district. These Christians
would be committed to reaching their members of Congress or other government officials on targeted issues that
affect hungry people. They envisioned a *citizens*

lobby—not a lobby of professionals in Washington, but of voters from the grassroots level—willing to advocate the cause of hungry people to their elected representatives in the government.

Bread for the World has now grown to a membership of 37,000 and provides a vehicle through which Christians can offer their gift of citizenship for the sake of the hungry both in the United States and abroad. With the help of a national staff, Bread for the World members seek to increase their understanding of hunger and its causes, listen to the poor, keep informed on the hunger situation in various parts of the world, follow development at the United Nations, and stay up-to-date on what is happening in the United States capital as it relates to hungry people.

Bread for the World

Bread for the World has been instrumental in the formulation and passage of such legislation as the following:

1. **The "Right to Food" resolution (a Sense of Congress Resolution which affirmed the right of every person to a nutritionally adequate diet and saw this right as a cornerstone of U.S. policy)**
2. **The U.S. grain reserve provision of the U.S. Farm Bill of 1977 (the reserve will help to avoid famines and stabilize the price of grain)**
3. **Extension of the Senate Select Committee on Nutrition and Human Needs**
4. **The grant back provision enabling countries that receive food aid to keep repayments when used for small-farm development**
5. **The depoliticizing of food assistance**
6. **The targeting of more development aid to the very poor**

The strength and effectiveness of Bread for the World resides at the local level. The national staff provides information and may target legislation and issues, but it is the communication of local groups with their elected representatives that makes the movement work.

Members are kept informed on hunger-related issues facing the U.S. Congress by a monthly newsletter. Other resources such as background papers, study courses, and books are also published to provide in-depth understanding of hunger issues. A special program for congregational hunger action groups—the Covenant Church program—has recently been developed to help these groups grow in knowledge and ability to act to combat hunger.

Bread for the World is one way church members in the United States may increase their understanding of the issues perpetuating hunger and act with others to address them. Perhaps similar groups in other countries are springing up. With groups like Bread for the World, Saints can share in an effort to leaven—with Christian values—the political, economic, and social structures which presently degrade and deprive millions of human lives.

Conclusion

In this chapter the author has described several corporate responses to hunger in which pastoral units (congregations) and/or individuals may participate. There are many other possibilities. One additional suggestion should be included here. Some pastoral units may want to form hunger task force groups. Such groups could initiate and coordinate all hunger responses within the pastoral unit including: (a) sponsoring a study program of hunger-related issues, (b) organizing support for the World Hunger Fund and Outreach International through such events as a hunger banquet, fast-a-thons, hike-a-thons, or community programs related to hunger, (c) developing and using materials relating to world hunger in corporate worship, (d) forming working coalitions with other groups in the community for such purposes as surveying the community to discover local hunger, and establishing a food bank, (e) encouraging support of scholarship funds to educate persons in Third World countries in agriculture, health, or community development (such as the International Education Fund), (f) inviting guest speakers from Outreach International, Bread for the World, or some other world hunger organization, (g) sponsoring a community forum on world hunger to which congregational representatives are invited, (h) establishing a pastoral unit library of hunger resources, and (i) investigating other responses appropriate for the pastoral unit. A task force could also invite families and individuals to share with the pastoral unit their personal responses to hunger which they engage in at home.

The church is called as a corporate body to act on behalf of the poor and hungry in the manner that was exemplified by our Lord. The *work intrusted to all* includes transforming those structures and relationships in the world which rob some persons of the elements essential to life and health. New life awaits the whole body as we help and heal those among us who suffer.

Reflection and Discussion Questions

1. What does stewardship mean to you? Record your definition.

_____

_____

_____

_____

_____

2. What do you feel is the most important aspect of the World Hunger Program?

_____

3. What, in your opinion, is the role of the church in the politics of hunger? The individual church member's role?

Church's Role

_____

_____

_____

Individual Role

_____

_____

_____

4. Did Jesus ever do anything you might consider political? Please explain.
5. Discuss the scripture, "Repression of unnecessary wants is in harmony with the law of stewardship and becomes my people" (Doctrine and Covenants 147:5b). Tell of a recent experience when you practiced this.
6. Find out where the World Hunger Fund has been used recently (what countries) and what has been done. (For information, write: The World Hunger Committee, P.O. Box 1059, Independence, MO 64051.)

Action Suggestions

1. Have your group prepare a Sunday morning worship service related to world hunger. You may find some of the worship resources listed at the end of the

chapter to be helpful in your planning. Include an explanation of how members may support the church's World Hunger Program. Describe how the fund has been used.

_____

_____

_____

_____

_____

2. Hold a fast-a-thon for hunger. Ask a group of persons to fast for thirty hours (or however long you choose). Ask them to solicit sponsors who will donate a certain amount of money per hour of their fast. The group may want to meet at the church or someone's home for the duration of the fast during which they could discuss hunger issues, invite guest speakers, pray, view films, sing, or participate in other appropriate activities. Donate the money to the World Hunger Fund or Outreach International, or use it to start a community food bank at your church. Ask a member of your group to write an article about your fast-a-thon for the mid-month *Herald*.

3. Create a hunger bulletin board for your church. Post hunger issues in the news, newsletters from Outreach International, Bread for the World, or other hunger relief and advocacy agencies, a world map indicating with colored shading the areas of extensive hunger,

news briefs about local hunger, letters from missionaries working in Third World countries, a list of suggested changes in life-style, or other related material.

4. Suggest that your group donate some books on hunger to a local library. Volunteer to help set up a hunger display in the library.
5. Find out if there is a local Bread for the World or other world hunger group in your town. If so, ask a group representative to come and talk to your group.

Worship Suggestions

The leader may read or ask different members of the group to read all or some of the following scriptures:

And he said unto them, It is impossible for them who trust in riches, to enter into the kingdom of God; but he who forsaketh the things which are of this world, it is possible with God, that he should enter in. —Luke 18:27

No man can serve two masters, for either he will hate the one, and love the other; or else he will hold to the one and despise the other. Ye cannot serve God and Mammon. —Matthew 6:24

Then I looked again at all the injustice that goes on in this world. The oppressed were crying, and no one would help them. No one would help them, because their oppressors had power on their side. —Ecclesiastes 4:1

If you oppress poor people, you insult the God who made them; but kindness shown to the poor is an act of worship. —Proverbs 14:31 (TEV)

When thou makest a dinner, or a supper, call not thy friends, nor thy brethren, neither thy kinsmen, nor rich neighbors; lest they also bid thee again, and a recompense be made thee. But when thou makes a feast, call the poor, the maimed, the lame, the blind, And thou shalt be blessed; for they cannot recompense thee; for thou shalt be recompensed at the resurrection of the just. —Luke 14:12-14

Ask three persons to offer prayers in the following ways:

1. The first person prays for the church and its special mission to the poor and needy.
2. The second person prays for the nation and its responsibilities to the poor nations.
3. The third person prays for our world, for justice and peace within and between all nations.

Teacher's Guide

Learning Objectives

At the close of this session participants will be able to

1. explain how the concept of stewardship provides the basis for a way of life that recognizes the earth as the home of the whole human family, to be shared equitably among all.
2. describe the World Hunger Program of the church.
3. define the purpose of Outreach International and cite examples of the kinds of projects which have been supported to date.
4. define their view of a Christian's political responsibility.
5. describe the work of Bread for the World.
6. list the functions that might be performed by a pastoral unit hunger task force.

Recommended Procedure

1. Review any reports from the "Action Suggestions" of the last chapter.
2. Outline briefly the content of Chapter 5. You may want to use a chalkboard or flip chart.

3. Discuss the questions at the end of the chapter. If no one in the group can answer number six, give someone that assignment for some other time.
4. Help the group make plans to present a Sunday morning worship service related to world hunger, as explained in "Action Suggestion 1."
5. Suggest that your group sponsor a fast-a-thon. Discuss the possibilities listed under suggestion number two.
6. Ask for volunteers to carry out the other action suggestions.
7. Close the session with the recommended worship. (Or this may be used to open the session.) Ask several different people to read the suggested scriptures, and ask three people to be prepared to offer the three special prayers as suggested.

Resources Needed

Chalkboard or flip chart (optional), chalk, felt-tip markers

A duplex offering envelope to show group the Oblation World Hunger (OWH) notation

An Outreach International *Newsletter*

A Bread for the World *Newsletter*

Writing utensils

Additional Resources

Books

Mary Evelyn Jegen and Bruno Manno, *The Earth Is the Lord's,* Paulist Press, New York, 1978. Essays on stewardship.

Slide Presentation

"Outreach International—Ministry of Possibility," available from Outreach International, P.O. Box 223, Independence, Missouri 64051. Slides and cassette tape, showing the work of OI. Price: $50.00. Loan: free.

Reminder

Remember to invite your pastor to meet with your group at the next session to discuss the possibility of setting up a pastoral unit task force on world hunger as described in "Action Suggestion 1" of Chapter 6.

Notes

1. Howard S. Sheehy, Jr., "Outreach International," *Saints Herald*, August 1, 1979, p. 34.
2. "Policies and Application Procedures," Outreach International.
3. *Overcoming World Hunger: The Challenge Ahead*, Report of the U.S. Presidential Commission on World Hunger, March, 1980, p. 10.

CHAPTER 6

PERSONAL RESPONSES TO HUNGER

In the final analysis it is personal response that will determine whether or not anything will be done about world hunger. Every group or corporate effort is first an expression of concern on the part of one person. This is exciting. It is possible for each of us to become a catalyst to arouse others to join in action on behalf of the hungry. Our initiative may have far-reaching effects.

Office of Graphic Arts/ Barrie Smith

Now that we have spent five sessions considering the dimensions of hunger, it is time to translate knowledge into action. We are aware of some of the causes of hunger and can now see some of the changes that must occur for it to be eliminated. Our biggest challenge is to close the gap between *knowing* and *doing*.

The material we have covered thus far suggests that our personal responses to hunger may fall into several basic categories. These include (a) continued study of hunger issues, (b) active and informed participation in the political process and in the shaping of public policy, (c) support of church and other hunger and development programs, (d) appropriate life-style changes, and (e) a consistent spiritual discipline that reflects our concern for the poor and hungry, our hope for justice and peace, and our desire to take on kingdom-building responsibility consistent with scriptural instruction.

Continued Study

If you have studied this resource in a group, you have already begun a practice of meeting to learn about hunger. Consequently it may be easy to continue to meet to expand your knowledge of the problem. If you wish to continue your study, select one of the resources on hunger listed at the end of this chapter and use it as the focus for continued group sessions.

In addition, an individual could read one of the suggested resources and give a review to your whole congregation. With or without the group, continue your private study and keep abreast of hunger issues in the news. Consider being a guest speaker for other groups to share the knowledge you have acquired.

Bread for the World

Political Action

You have become aware that much of the suffering of the world's hungry begins in governmental chambers. Study existing laws and pending legislation which affect the hungry world. Focus on a particular issue and write a letter to the editor of your local newspaper. If possible mention the name of your legislator. This will bring your letter to his or her immediate attention.

Join a public policy advocacy organization and study the hunger-related legislation which it has targeted. Share your views concerning it. Find out what plans are under way to sponsor or support other legislation in favor of the hungry world. Be creative and suggest other ways public policies might address hunger.

Study the subject of the annual Bread for the World Offering of Letters. (This is a Sunday when you may accompany the usual monetary offering with an offering of personal letters to your legislator. Indicate your views on the targeted legislation and your concern that public policy be responsive to the needs of hungry people.) Suggest that your pastoral unit participate in the Offering of Letters.

Follow the work of the United Nations. Find out which bodies within the United Nations are most concerned with the problem of world hunger, food crises, development of land and natural resources, international investments, disaster relief, and so on.

Suggest that your pastoral unit sponsor the production of television or radio public service spots on hunger. Make use of local school media departments. Ask the local ministerial association to join with you to bring the problem of world hunger before the public.

Support of Church Hunger and Development Programs

Encourage your pastoral unit to establish a hunger task force. Help to get a continuing program of hunger education and action started. Recognize that a program to combat something as complex as hunger will require patient and persistent efforts.

Support the World Hunger Program of the church through regular contributions to the World Hunger Fund, using your duplex offering envelopes. Support the work of Outreach International. Contributions are already improving the lives of many needy persons around the world. Self-help development programs are promoting long-lasting and far-reaching emancipation from hunger and poverty.

Life-style

When we discussed the causes of hunger, one of the factors mentioned was the affluence explosion among the rich nations of the world. We consume far more than is just and fair in an age of hunger and starvation. We must find ways to simplify our lives. It is true that making changes in our life-styles may be difficult. Such changes run counter to the expectation and practice of our society. As one author stated:

Surroundings teach Christians, especially those of us in Western cultures, that more is better. We learn to measure our material lives by what we don't have, instead of by comparison with the stark needs of the rest of the world. Measuring wealth by what is absent destines us to an unclear perspective of our material well-being. Most of us can point to those who have so much materially that we are poor by comparison.

In terms of God's vision for the human family, this puts Christians in the role of seekers of resources, not sharers. We begin to see ourselves as poor because we do not have dishwashers, instead of wealthy because we have food to eat and dishes on which to serve it. The truth about our world is clouded by a life of seeking more, more, more.[1]

Take an inventory of your life-style by seriously considering the following questions with your family:

1. Discuss the things you need and all the things you have. What is your definition of *things you need?* How do you determine this?

2. What could you do without, so as to share with others who are in need? What appliances do you have that you could do without? How could you conserve energy and cut down on the use of imported luxury items? Do any of your habits demand products that can only be supplied by the nonfood agriculture of the hungry world?

3. How much food do you waste? How can you cut down on use of convenience foods that require excessive amounts of energy for processing and are low in nutritional value?

4. How many different people does your life-style affect directly? Indirectly?

5. How much time do you spend maintaining material possessions that could be spent serving others if you simplified your life-style?
6. How does your employment affect world hunger? Would you be willing to change jobs if you felt it would help the hungry?
7. What else could you do to live more faithfully and justly in the world?

Spiritual Discipline

Our efforts to overcome hunger and poverty should include prayer. "The effectual fervent prayer of a righteous (person) availeth much" (James 5:16). This scripture identifies prayer as a working force, an act that brings things to pass that would otherwise not occur. It tells us that prayer is something that works. A contrast is often drawn between praying and working. One church school director who called upon a class member to pray received the reply, "I am not a praying Christian, I am a working Christian." The thoughtful reflection of the director was, "But praying is working. It is the most effective work that anyone can do; that is, we can often bring more to pass by praying than we can by any other form of effort we might put forth.... Real praying is a costly exercise but it pays far more than it costs. It is not easy work but it is the most profitable of all work. We can accomplish more by time and strength put into prayer than we can by putting the same amount of time and strength into anything else."[2]

The fact that Jesus spent so much time in prayer suggests that this assessment of the effect of prayer is accurate. As we dare to work for a world free from poverty and hunger we know that we do not enter this struggle alone. In believing that God will hear us, we should accompany our efforts to combat hunger with daily prayer for the poor and hungry. We may want to follow some of these prayer suggestions:

- Every day bring the reality of hungry people to our Lord.
- Listen to their cries and hear the voice of the Lord.
- Try to discern what God is telling us in their voices. Ask God's direction in determining our role in responding to their need.
- Petition the Lord to liberate those who are captives of riches and selfishness.
- Pray for the transformation of oppressive structures that prevent human development.
- Ask God's blessing on those who work among the poor and hungry in the name of Christ.
- Pray that all peoples of the earth will learn to live together in peace and unity.

To pray is something we can do each day in our hearts. It is also something we can do as a family or faith community. Keep the cause of the poor and hungry among the prayers of petition in your pastoral unit life.

As we begin to carry out responses within each of the categories we have been discussing, we will see that this is all a part of our responsibility as stewards over our gifts. The wise and faithful use of God's gifts, for the purposes God has designed, leads us to freedom and discovery. As we use these resources for their intended purposes, we are freed from the bondage of overaccumulation and find sharing to be a freeing, fulfilling experience. We find

our personal gifts expanding as we pour them out for others.

We also begin to discover the essential unity and sacredness of the whole universe. The kingdom way of life acknowledges that unity and contributes to it. The oneness that results exalts the individual being of each member. In contrast, brokenness and lack of fulfillment characterize a world made up of rich and poor, and this demeans life, rather than exalting it.

Perhaps the most critical part of stewardship of self is the need to think creatively of the future. We must envision a future that is very different from our past if we are to survive the dangers which threaten the world today. As followers of Jesus Christ we are a minority in the world. But if we will renew our efforts to act upon our faith, close the gap between knowing and doing, think and act creatively and courageously at this juncture in time, then we may shape a new world in which justice and peace will prevail and no one will go hungry.

Reflection and Discussion Questions

1. Explain the ways in which group members can strengthen and reinforce one another's personal responses to hunger.

2. How can you share what you have learned with others (a) at home, (b) at church, (c) in the community. List your ideas below.

At Home

_____

_____

_____

At Church

_____

_____

_____

In the Community

_____

_____

_____

3. Make plans for further study/action by brainstorming among yourselves, then selecting one or two ideas to carry out.

Action Suggestions

1. Invite your pastor to meet with the group and discuss the possibility of establishing a task force on hunger.

2. As a group visit an agency in your town that works with poor people. Arrange for interviews with the staff to determine the cause of poverty and hunger in your area. (Formulate your interview questions in advance.) Discuss with your group ways that you may support the work of such an agency.

3. Ask a member of your group to visit other churches in your community to find out what they are doing about world hunger, then report back to the group.

4. Request two or three members of your group to plan ways to involve the children in your pastoral unit in responses to world hunger.

Worship Suggestions

In the spirit of commission the group leader may read the following:

> I give unto you to be the salt of the earth; but if the salt shall lose its savor, wherewith shall the earth be salted? the salt shall thenceforth be good for nothing, but to be cast out, and to be trodden under foot of men. I give unto you to be the light of the world; a city that is set on a hill cannot be hid. Behold, do men light a candle and put it under a bushel? Nay, but on a candlestick; and it giveth light to all that are in the house. Therefore, let your light so shine before this world, that they may see your good works, and glorify your Father who is in heaven. —Matthew 5:15-18

Acting out of an increased awareness of hunger, its causes, and the responses we are called to make, ask the group to share in reading together the Shakertown Pledge:[3]

Recognizing that the earth and the fullness thereof is a gift from our gracious God, and that we are called to cherish, nurture, and provide loving stewardship for the earth's resources, and recognizing that life itself is a gift, and a call to responsibility, joy, and celebration, I make the following declarations:

1. I declare myself to be a world citizen.
2. I commit myself to lead an ecologically sound life.
3. I commit myself to lead a life of creative simplicity and to share my personal wealth with the world's poor.
4. I commit myself to join with others in reshaping institutions in order to bring about a more just global society in which all persons have full access to the needed resources for their physical, emotional, intellectual, and spiritual growth.
5. I commit myself to occupational accountability, and in so doing I will seek to avoid the creation of products which cause harm to others.
6. I affirm the gift of my body, and commit myself to its proper nourishment and physical well-being.
7. I commit myself to examine continually my relations with others, and to attempt to relate honestly, morally, and lovingly to those around me.
8. I commit myself to personal renewal through prayer, meditation and study.
9. I commit myself to responsible participation in a community of faith.

Close with a circle prayer.

Teacher's Guide

Learning Objectives

At the close of this session participants will be able to

1. list several basic categories into which their personal reponses to world hunger may fall.
2. identify several specific responses within each cate-

gory that members of the group may want to adopt.

3. choose from among several options the personal responses to hunger that are appropriate for each person.

Overview of Chapter 6

Chapter 6 contains challenges for persons to put into action the knowledge they have gained by commitment to a personal response to world hunger. It is suggested that possible responses fall into several basic categories, and various responses within each category are discussed. The whole chapter is a call to action. Students are urged to think creatively of the future and accept responsibility to shape a new world order in which justice and peace will prevail.

Recommended Procedure

1. Review progress on the "Action Suggestions" from the last session. Ask if the groups need any help.
2. Summarize the content of Chapter 6. Encourage students to discuss the life-style inventory with their families. Suggest that students make the prayer suggestions that are listed a part of their daily prayer list.
3. Discuss the questions at the end of the chapter.
4. View filmstrip No. 4, "Personal Responses," from the filmstrip kit, "A World Hungry." You may want to view No. 5, "More Personal Responses," if there is time.
5. Discuss with your pastor the possibility of establishing a pastoral unit task force on hunger. Be sure to allow sufficient time for this, or plan a

separate time for this purpose. If you prefer, after discussing it as a group, ask for volunteers who will work closely with him in getting this started.

6. Invite the class to go as a group to a local agency as described in "Action Suggestion 2." You may want to make a report of this visit to your pastoral unit. Your group may want to investigate ways of supporting the work of the agency in the local community.

7. Lead the group in the closing worship and close with circle prayer.

Resources Needed

Filmstrip No. 4, "Personal Responses," from "A World Hungry," available from Audio-Visual Library, the Auditorium, P.O. Box 1059, Independence, MO, U.S.A.
Filmstrip projector
Cassette player
Screen
Writing utensils

Additional Resources

Books

Larry Minear, *New Hope for the Hungry?*, Friendship Press, New York, 1975, ch. 6.

Gerald and Patricia Mische, *Toward a Human World Order*, Paulist Press, New York, 1977, chapters 12 and 13.

Ronald J. Sider, *Cry Justice, The Bible on Hunger and Poverty*, Paulist Press, New York, 1980.

Films

"More Personal Responses," Filmstrip No. 5 from "A World Hungry."

Notes

1. *Leaven*, Bread for the World Covenant Church Quarterly, Vol. II, No. 2, p. 4.
2. R. A. Torrey, *The Power of Prayer*, Zondervan Publishing House, 1980, p. 28.
3. The Shakertown Pledge Group, South Minneapolis, Minnesota.

EVALUATION FORM
Hunger and Discipleship

Each teacher and participant is requested to complete questions 1-14. *In addition, each teacher is requested to complete the remainder of the questions.* Please check only one blank for each question.

1. In what type of class or setting was this resource used?
   ____Church School   ____Personal study   ____Other_____

2. What was the age category of the class?
   ____Senior High   ____Young Adult   ____Middle Adult
   ____Senior Adults   ____Mixed

3. If all or part of the time was spent in mixed groups, how would you describe the experience?
   ____Very fulfilling   ____Good   ____Fair
   ____Not at all helpful   ____Other _____
   Comments: _____

4. What was the approximate class size?
   ____1-10   ____11-25   ____26-50   ____50 +

5. What is your general reaction to the resource?
   ____Enthusiastic   ____Accepting   ____Used with reservation
   ____Unaccepting   ____Other _____
   Comments: _____

6. How would you rate the difficulty of the reading materials?
   ____Too difficult   ____About right   ____Too easy

7. How do you react to the following statement? The issues considered in the resource represent vital concerns that Christians everywhere should do something about.
   ____Strongly agree   ____Agree   ____Disagree
   ____Strongly disagree
   Comments: _____

8. Do you think the Action Suggestions proved to be helpful in learning more about the problem of world hunger and in actually doing something about it?
   ____Yes   ____No   ____Not sure
   Comments: _____

9. How would you rate the material in both *informing* and *equipping* you to become involved in solutions related to world hunger?
   ____Very helpful   ____Somewhat helpful   ____Not helpful
   Comments: _____

10. Are the learning objectives and the chapter summaries clearly stated and understandable?
    ____Yes   ____No   ____Not sure

11. How helpful were the Reflection and Discussion Questions in assisting you to explore different aspects of each chapter?
    ____Very helpful   ____Somewhat helpful   ____Not helpful
    Comments: _____

12. If you feel there was a particularly helpful Action Suggestion or Reflection and Discussion Question, please identify the number _____ and page _____.

Comments: _____

13. If you feel there was a particularly unhelpful Action Suggestion or Reflection and Discussion Question, please identify the number _____ and page _____.

Comments: _____

14. What other comments do you have regarding the resource?

_____

_____

_____

_____

_____

For the teacher only

15. Were the resources adequate in helping to prepare for each study session?

_____Quite adequate   _____Adequate   _____Inadequate

16. How much time did you spend with your group studying each chapter?

_____Less than one hour   _____Between one and two hours

_____More than two hours

17. How helpful did you find the Recommended Procedure to be in your study sessions?

_____Very helpful   _____Helpful   _____Not helpful

18. How would you rate the reaction of the students to the resource?

_____Enthusiastic   _____Accepting   _____Reserved

_____Unaccepting   _____Other

19. How helpful were the Worship Suggestions?

_____Very helpful   _____Helpful   _____Not helpful

20. Would you like to see additional resources produced on this subject?

_____Yes   _____No   _____Not sure

Please mail to:
The Zionic Relations Office
The Auditorium
P.O. Box 1059
Independence, MO 64051